David's
Vegan
Home Cooking

David's Vegan
Home Cooking

David A. Gabbe

Evergreen Northwest

www.DavidsVeganKitchen.com

The information and recipes in this book are not intended to furnish medical advice. Please consult your health care provider for advice on any specific health problems you have.

Cover design and layout by Patrick Floresca

Library of Congress Cataloging-in-Publication Data
Gabbe, David A.
  David's Vegan Home Cooking/David A. Gabbe
     p.   cm.
  Includes index.
  ISBN 978-0-9718052-2-4
  1. Vegan cookery I. Title
TX837.G 2011
641.5'636-dc21   2011090971

Printed in the United States of America

10 9 8 7 6 5 4 3 2

First Edition

Contents

Acknowledgements

A book is like a home. Many hands play a role in its construction. My thanks to all who helped make it what it is.

I'd like to thank all of the students I've fed over the past 20 years, too numerous to name, who sampled many of these recipes and offered excellent suggestions. You allowed me to see that people of all dietary persuasions love good healthy food.

A heartfelt thanks to the following organizations for their tireless work in promoting a safe and healthy diet and for seeking to fill our hearts with compassion not towards animals only, but towards all human beings: American Vegan Society, North American Vegetarian Society, People for the Ethical Treatment of Animals, Physicians Committee for Responsible Medicine, United Poultry Concerns, Farm Sanctuary, and Vegetarian Resource Group.

A big thank you to these "local" groups providing education and support to anyone interested in issues of healthy diet and lifestyle: NW VEG (Portland), EVEN (Eugene), and Veg of WA (Seattle).

Thanks to all of you at *Vegetarian Times* and *VegNews* magazines for helping publicize the wondrous bounty of plant-based cooking.

To *The Oregonian*, my newspaper here in Portland, goes my thanks for its salubrious treatment of all things vegetarian and vegan. Especially, I appreciate its featuring an enlightened and practical vegan column in the food section.

Thank you to my kids (really, not kids anymore) for help in proofreading the manuscript. When I think about you both, I'm convinced I'm one of the luckiest fathers on the planet.

To my mother, an "elderly" Pennsylvanian still young in her 90's, my deepest thanks for, as a young widow, singlehandedly raising three children, and for instilling in us an abiding concern for all those in need.

I am grateful to my wife Carolyn, not only for her invaluable input in this and everything I do, but for being my partner in this grand life adventure, now going on 35 years.

A final thanks to all of you who go out and work in any way you can to create a more vegan world.

> *"First we receive the light,*
> *then we impart it.*
> *Thus we repair the world."*
> —The Kabbalah

Preface

Vegetarians, like most people, eat lots of things: grains, beans, nuts and seeds, vegetables, fruits, dairy products, and eggs—but not meat, poultry, or fish. Some people called "vegans," go further and refrain from eating dairy, eggs, and honey, too—and also strive to avoid the use of all animal products, wherever they may be found.

And many who refrain from the flesh of living creatures do so because of health reasons. Overwhelming evidence links the consumption of animal products with heart disease, cancers, diabetes, obesity, and a number of other serious conditions.

This book follows the vegan lifestyle I have led for many years. Why do I pursue a diet that includes a wide variety of plant-based foods, and eliminates all animal products? Because, it's the diet most conducive to vibrant health and increased longevity. It's also the diet kindest to animals and least demanding of our planet's resources.

A century of nutrition research has made it exceedingly clear that a simple, whole foods diet based on vegetables, beans, whole grains, fruits, seeds, and nuts can do what the most powerful tools of medical science cannot do—prevent or favorably resolve many types of cancer, as well as stop heart disease in its tracks.

The recipes in this book are original and have come about through my life experience as a vegan of many years, and from the kitchens of the many cooking classes I have taught. The dishes are low-fat, gluten-free, and cholesterol-free, and use only whole grains and other unrefined foods. And, they're quick to fix and taste good, too!

As you scan the recipes in this book, you may notice that I have not included a nutritional analysis for any of the dishes. I have refrained from doing so because I believe optimum health can be achieved by avoiding all animal products and by eating a wide variety of whole, plant-based foods.

You won't find cholesterol, gluten, white sugar, white flour—or any other nutritional disasters in these recipes. Adopting a vegan diet is an act of liberation. You need not be concerned with counting calories, carbohydrate grams, portions, cholesterol, or saturated fat amounts. Having to eat with one eye all the time on the numbers and nutrients is no way to live.

Just as we should eat whole foods, instead of fractured and refined foods, so should we look at how healthful a vegan diet can be when taken as a whole—without having to analyze each and every ingredient or recipe.

Unofficial polls of my own students convince me that more and more people want general directions—a "big-picture" view—on how best to go about adopting a wholesome, plant-based diet, instead of a nutritional analysis of each meal component.

A vegan diet is naturally low in fat and sodium, high in complex carbohydrates, free of cholesterol, full of fiber and nutrients, endowed with protein, and brimming with vitamins and minerals.

These recipes reflect good old home cooking. Here are everyday meals, not banquet fare. Yet, at a deeper level, these low-fat, plant-based dishes are truly celebrations—celebrations of life, of compassion, of wisdom in realizing that with each bite we are being well-fed, healthy, and kind.

Here's a little global perspective. The production of meat requires that tens of millions of tons of fossil fuels and millions of acres of tropical forest be burned each year. The resultant enormous amount of carbon dioxide and methane released into the atmosphere contributes significantly to planetary climate change and to the destructive weather extremes that follow.

It should also be pointed out the sheer waste and inefficiency of meat production. Take the soybean. It's a complete protein as high in quality as meat. Twenty times more protein can be obtained from one acre of land planted with soybeans, than from one acre that's grazing cattle. While a growing number of children die of malnutrition and starvation around the world each year, cattle populations are increasing and consuming enormous amounts of grain and bean products—food that could be fed directly to people.

A commitment to a plant-based diet is the most powerful condemnation you can make against world hunger.

Here is a path, a daily reminder of what truly nourishes us. To change the type of food we will now eat is to begin a sublime journey. And, the pleasure is all in the journey. There is no end.

Increasingly, people are discovering that there are few things that will have a more profound and positive effect on their lives than adopting a healthy vegan diet. I dedicate this book to all who strive for such unparalleled well-being and inner-peace.

1 Some Basics

Daily Healthy Eating Guide

The vegan diet most conducive to good health includes a wide variety of vegetables, legumes, whole grains, fruits, seeds, and nuts. Important to remember is to focus on variety.

Studies show that those people who follow a varied plant-based diet can expect to lose excess body weight, normalize blood pressure and cholesterol level, improve or resolve diabetes, reduce overall cancer risk, and even reverse coronary atherosclerosis. Until recently, reversing heart disease was thought a medical impossibility.

The guidelines that follow provide general information on a plant-based diet. Keep in mind that nutritional requirements can vary based on differences in body size, condition, and level of activity. All daily nutritional needs can be met on the following plan, except vitamin B12 and vitamin D.

The body makes vitamin D from sunlight, assuming that adequate sun exposure is received. There are many variables involved in determining that sun exposure. These should be researched before making a choice on how best to obtain vitamin D. A good place to start is www.drmcdougall.com.

For those people choosing vitamin D supplementation, there are two forms of vitamin D. Vitamin D2 is a vegan product made from yeast while vitamin D3 is made from lanolin obtained from sheep's wool. Vitamin D2 has been shown to be as effective as vitamin D3 in preventing vitamin D deficiency.

Vitamin B12 is found in many fortified foods (check labels) and in "Red Star" nutritional yeast. It is also available in supplement form.

Raising Vegan Children

Not only **can** children be raised on a plant-based diet, they **should** be! Starting a new human being off on a well-planned, vegan diet bestows a gift of vibrant health that will be appreciated for a lifetime.

The American Dietetic Association states that appropriately planned vegan diets satisfy the nutrient needs of all stages of life, including infancy, childhood, and adolescence. Such a diet is ideal for the young athlete, as well.

To learn the simple and sound guidelines for raising vegan children, pick up a copy of *Raising Vegetarian Children* by Joanne Stepaniak, M.S. Ed., and Vesanto Melina, M.S., R.D. (2002). Additional invaluable information can be obtained by visiting the website of the Vegetarian Resource Group at www.VRG.org.

Daily Recommendations

Vegetables

4 cups or more of raw vegetables or 2 cups or more of cooked. Include such nutrient-dense vegetables as leafy greens, cruciferous vegetables (i.e. collards, kale, broccoli, and bok choy), sweet potatoes, carrots, and cabbage.

Beans, Peas, and Lentils

½ cup to 1 cup of cooked beans. Include all kinds of beans, such as navy, lima, black, kidney, garbanzo (chickpea), and pinto. Also include lentils, split speas, and black-eyed peas.

Soyfoods

4-6 ounces of firm or extra-firm tofu, or 3-4 ounces of tempeh, or ½ cup to 1 cup of cooked soybeans.

Whole Grains

2½ cups or more of cooked whole grains. Include such whole grains as brown rice, millet, buckwheat, quinoa, rolled oats, wild rice, and amaranth. (A slice of whole-grain bread or ½ cup cooked whole-grain pasta is each equivalent to ½ cup cooked whole grains.)

Fruit

3 or more pieces of fresh fruit. Include citrus fruits, apples, pears, bananas, peaches, kiwis, and equal-sized portions of berries and melons. ½ cup of cooked fruit equals 1 piece of fresh fruit.

Nuts and Seeds

2 tablespoons flax seed meal and 3-4 tablespoons of chopped walnuts. (Flax meal contains significant amounts of anti-cancer fibrous compounds; walnuts are rich in anti-inflammatory and heart-healthy fatty acids.) Include optional small amounts of seeds such as sesame, pumpkin, sunflower, and nuts such as almonds, filberts, and cashews. Small amounts of nut butters may also be included.

Oils

Up to 1 tablespoon each of flax seed oil and coconut oil. (Flax seed oil contains powerful anti-inflammatory fatty acids; coconut oil contains remarkable immune-enhancing compounds.) Include optional small amounts of such other oils as olive or sesame oil.

Sample Menus

The following sample menus are chock full of protein and essential nutrients. As noted earlier, be sure to consider how vitally important it is to add flax seed meal, flax seed oil, coconut oil, and walnuts. (And, don't forget the importance of vitamin B12 and vitamin D.)

Breakfast
Day 1: *Flax-Date Granola* with non-dairy milk and fresh fruit

Day 2: *Rice Date Smoothie* and fresh fruit

Day 3: *Creamy Oatmeal* and fresh fruit

Lunch
Day 1: *Tangy Black Beans* on *Basic Brown Rice*, and *Rainbow Salad*

Day 2: *Split Pea Soup*, *Basic Quinoa*, and steamed broccoli

Day 3: *Tofu Scrambled 'Eggs' & Greens*, *Bagel*, *and* green salad

Snack
Day 1: *Apple Bread*, *'Mozzarella Nut Cheese'*, and fresh fruit

Day 2: *Millet Pudding* and fresh fruit

Day 3: *Rice Garbo Bars* and fresh fruit or vegetable sticks

Dinner
Day 1: *Tempeh 'Meatloaf'*, *Basic Buckwheat*, and *Collard 'Spaghetti'*

Day 2: *Tofu 'Cutlets'*, *4-Grain Fusion*, and *Steamed Veggie Salad*

Day 3: *Bean Burritos*, *Basic Brown Rice*, and green salad

Dessert
Day 1: *Apple Blueberry Cobbler* or fresh fruit

Day 2: *Chocolate Chip Cookies* or fresh fruit

Day 3: *Fruity 'Jell-o'* or fresh fruit

Transitioning

Whether your goal is to embrace a plant-based lifestyle, or simply to add healthier dishes to the menu, switching to animal-free dining is easier than you think. Most of your favorite meals have vegan counterparts that will astound you not only with how delicious they are, but with how much fun you'll have exploring new foods.

Trade in your usual meals for these vegan replacements and you'll leave behind excess protein, saturated animal fat, and cholesterol. In exchange, you'll partake in meals rich in protective plant compounds (phytochemicals), low in fat, free of cholesterol, and full of fiber.

Replace scrambled eggs and sausages
with *Tofu Scrambled 'Eggs'* and *Tempeh Breakfast 'Sausages'*

Replace boxed cereal and milk
with *Kasha Krunch Cereal* or *Flax-Date Granola* and non-dairy milk

Replace French toast with butter and syrup
with *Tofu French Toast* and *Cinnamon Maple Glaze*

Replace donuts or bagels
with *Cinnamon Sticky Buns* or *'Sourdough' Bagels*

Replace chicken sandwich with mayonnaise and potato chips
with *Tofu 'Cutlets'* with *Tofu 'Mayo'* and *Roasted Potato Rounds*

Replace beef burritos, pizza, or meat lasagna
with *Bean Burritos*, *Pizza with 'Cheddar'*, or *Navy 'Lasagna'*

Replace chicken noodle soup or clam chowder
with *Tofu 'Chicken' Noodle Soup* or *Corn Chowder*

Replace chicken fajitas and piña colada
with *Tempeh 'Fajitas'* and *'Piña Colada'* (alcohol-free)

Replace pork fried rice or sushi filled with tuna
with *Tofu 'Egg Fried' Rice* or *'Sushi'* filled with tofu

Replace chocolate cake or brownies
with *Chocolate (Broccoli) Cake* or *Chocolate Brownies*

Stocking the Vegan Pantry

It's certainly easier to plan and prepare wholesome meals when you've got a variety of quality foods on hand. Here's a list of ingredients and products I use in my own kitchen. You could go out and buy them all at once (they would always remember you at that store!). Or, look over some of the recipes in this book and make a modest list of things to shop for.

With any number of the following staples on hand you'll be able to put together many simple, nourishing and delicious meal ideas found in this book. Remember—you don't need them all to get started.Be sure to check the expiration dates on the jars or other packaging when purchasing soyfoods, flours, and nut and seed butters.

Produce: A seasonally-adjusted assortment of fresh vegetables and fruit. Include carrots, sweet potatoes and yams, collard greens, kale, broccoli, bok choy, leaf lettuce, cabbage, beets, onions, tomatoes, cauliflower, eggplant, fresh ginger, fresh garlic, apples, pears, bananas, citrus fruit, grapes, peaches, melons, and berries.

Legumes: Garbanzo beans, black beans, pinto beans, navy beans, black-eyed peas, lima beans, kidney beans, soybeans, split peas, and lentils. Dried beans are kept in airtight containers in a cool, dry spot away from light and used within 6 months of purchase.

Soyfoods: Tofu, tempeh, soy sauce, miso, soy milk, and soy yogurt. Tempeh is best kept in the freezer until needed, up to 3 months after purchase. Tofu, soy milk, and soy yogurt are kept in the refrigerator and should be used within 10 days of opening. Soy sauce (after opening) and miso are refrigerated and good for 6 months.

Grains: Brown rice (long and short-grain), millet, buckwheat, quinoa, wild rice, amaranth, rolled oats, and whole oats. Also, tortillas (brown rice and whole corn), whole-grain crackers, brown rice cakes, and unrefined corncakes. Uncooked whole grains are kept in airtight containers or bags in the refrigerator and used within 6 months of purchase. Tortillas are kept in the refrigerator and used within 2 weeks of purchase, or frozen for a longer period.

Flours: Oat flour (homemade and store-bought), brown rice flour, millet flour (homemade), garbanzo bean flour, cornmeal (unrefined), and coconut flour (homemade). These whole-grain flours are kept in airtight containers in the refrigerator and used within 3 months of purchase or of being home made.

Pastas: Dried noodles in a variety of shapes and sizes. Made with either brown rice flour or 100% buckwheat flour, and sometimes unrefined corn flour or quinoa flour. Dried pasta is stored in airtight containers in a cool, dry spot and used within 1 year of purchase.

Nuts, Seeds, and "Butters": Variety of raw nuts and seeds, including almonds, walnuts, cashews, pecans, filberts (hazelnuts), sunflower seeds, and sesame seeds. Peanut butter, almond butter, tahini, and cashew butter. Nuts and seeds are stored in airtight containers in the refrigerator or freezer and used within 6 months of purchase. All opened jars of nut butters are kept in the refrigerator and used within 3 months.

Dried Fruits: Raisins, dates, apricots, figs, and prunes are kept in airtight containers in the refrigerator and used within 6 months.

Oils: Flax seed oil, olive oil (extra-virgin), canola oil, toasted sesame oil, coconut oil, and non-dairy margarine. All opened bottles or jars of oil, except flax seed oil and coconut oil, are refrigerated and used within 6 months of purchase. Flax seed oil should be kept in the refrigerator, either opened or un-opened, and used within 6 weeks of opening. Coconut oil is not refrigerated and should be used within 1 year of opening.

Sweeteners: Liquid sweeteners include maple syrup, brown rice syrup, agave nectar, and blackstrap molasses. Dry sweetener is sugar (i.e. evaporated cane juice). All opened liquid sweeteners are kept in the refrigerator and used within 3 months of opening.

Condiments: Vinegars (including apple cider, brown rice, and balsamic), prepared mustard, liquid smoke, mirin, sea salt, dill pickles, jelly (fruit spread), extracts (vanilla, lemon, and orange). Refrigerate opened jars of mustard, pickles, and jelly. All others are kept in a cool spot.

Herbs and Spices (dried): Garlic powder, onion powder, black pepper, cinnamon, turmeric, parsley, thyme, basil, cumin, cayenne pepper, ginger, paprika, curry powder, chili powder, red pepper flakes, dill, chives, oregano, and sage. Kept in cool, dark, and dry spot. Used with best flavor within 3 months of opening.

Frozen Items: Fruit juice concentrates (apple, orange, etc.), corn kernels, berries, peas, sprouted-grain bread, non-dairy ice cream, flax seed meal (homemade), lemon and lime juices (homemade).

Other: Dried mushrooms, sun-dried tomatoes, nutritional yeast flakes, cocoa powder, carob powder, nori, arrowroot powder, tapioca, agar, poppy seeds, caraway seeds, baking powder, dried coconut, non-dairy chocolate chips, instant coffee (granules or powder), teas (green and herbal), roasted red pepper, and pasta sauce. All are kept in airtight containers in a cool, dark spot. Opened jars of the last two products are refrigerated and used within 3 weeks.

Equipping the Vegan Kitchen

I have found the following equipment to be essential to my kitchen:

Pots: Four stainless steel pots and lids. One each in the following sizes: 8 quart, 4 quart, 3 quart, and 1 quart. The largest one is ideal for cooking large batches of beans, grains, and pasta, while the 4 quart pot nicely handles smaller quantities of these things. The smaller pots are great for cooking and reheating small dishes. Each pot could double as a skillet, too. The larger pots are often called "stockpots" and the smaller ones sometimes called "saucepans."

Skillet: A 12" non-stick skillet (and lid) allows me to cook with little or no oil. It is a heavy skillet of good-quality, non-stick construction.

Knives: Three good-quality knives are a must. A chef's (or cook's) knife (8") for chopping and slicing. A small paring knife for coring and trimming, and a serrated knife (with a blade like a saw) that's ideal for slicing tomatoes, sushi, soft-skinned fruits, and breads.

Measuring Cups: Liquid measuring cups in 1 and 2 cup sizes. I prefer not to use the dry measuring cups. A 1 cup liquid measuring cup has the same volume as a 1 cup dry measuring cup, and so all ingredients, wet or dry, can be measured in a liquid measuring cup. I measure all ingredients, wet or dry, using liquid measuring cups.

Measuring Spoons: I have two sets. Each set comes with spoons in 1 tablespoon, 1 teaspoon, ½ teaspoon, and ¼ teaspoon sizes.

Cutting Boards: Two large cutting boards. One for garlic, onions, and other savory or pungent items. Another board for fruit and sweet things. I wash them thoroughly after each use. When my cutting boards get well-worn and filled with grooves and scratches (which can harbor bacteria), I replace them.

Mixing Bowls: One 8 cup mixing bowl and several smaller ones.

Baking Dishes and Pans: 8x8" and 9x13" glass baking dishes and similar-sized metal square and rectangular baking pans; 9" glass pie plate; small 3x6" metal loaf pans; and muffin tins. I find useful a quality, non-stick jelly roll pan (basically a cookie sheet with low rim) which is ideal for cookies, wet batters, and all kinds of savory baking jobs. Also, glass casserole dishes (small and large) with covers.

Baking Sheets: One large, good-quality non-stick "cookie" sheet.

Other Invaluable Kitchen Tools: Grater, strainers, apple corer, peeler, spatulas (metal, non-metal, and rubber), rolling pin, wire rack, steamer basket, wooden spoons, soup ladle, cheesecloth (un-bleached), large slotted spoons, serving spoons, citrus hand juicer (glass), salad spinner, salad bowl, blender, and toaster oven.

Protein, Calcium, and Iron

A vegan is often asked: "If you don't eat any animal products, where do you get your protein, calcium, and iron?"

Protein

A person who eats a variety of legumes (beans, peas, or lentils), whole grains, vegetables, fruits, and seeds or nuts each day and consumes enough calories to at least maintain his/her ideal, healthy body weight, will completely satisfy the need for protein. And every meal does not have to contain such a variety of foods, nor is it necessary to combine foods, such as beans and grains, at each meal. Eating a variety of whole foods each day will provide all the high quality essential amino acids (protein) needed for good health.

The body's need for protein is quite modest. The recommended dietary allowances (RDA) are 60-65 grams of protein each day for adult males, and 50 grams for adult females. However, the RDA are considered far too high by many scientists and nutritionists. They contend that humans require as little as 30 grams of protein daily. They cite the fact that mother's milk is only 5% protein—and it meets the requirements of an infant whose growth rate and protein needs are greater than at any other time in life.

Therefore, the official recommendations for protein could be almost twice the amount actually needed. It turns out that the RDA are intentionally inflated, containing a very generous built-in safety factor to cover everyone—even those rare persons who need large amounts of protein. It would seem then, that average Americans are being advised to consume much more protein than necessary. And Americans comply by eating at least twice—and often three to four times—the amount of protein actually needed.

So what's wrong with eating too much protein? Whatever protein the body does not need has to be broken down and gotten rid of. The body will burn a bit of protein for energy, store some as fat, and struggle to eliminate all the rest—putting a hefty strain on the kidneys, in the process. There's another problem with eating all that protein—most of which comes from animals. It has to do with osteoporosis.

Animal protein—such has beef, chicken, eggs, pork, fish, and cheese—is quite high in amino acids, and, when digested, causes the blood to become acidic. In order to neutralize the acid, your body dissolves calcium from your own bones and pumps it into the blood. Then, the calcium in the blood passes through the kidneys and is excreted in the urine. The more animal protein eaten, the more acid dumped in the blood, and the more calcium is lost from your bones.

And, the end of that road could be osteoporosis.

On the other hand, eating plant protein does not cause calcium loss. In part, that's because plant protein contains far less amino acids than does animal protein. Also, animal protein contains sulfur (plants have none) which plays an aggressive role in causing calcium loss.

With all that calcium being filtered through the kidneys, these vital organs sometimes literally wear out long before their time. The result is kidney disease. Sometimes, the result is kidney stones—which are made of calcium lost from your bones.

There is yet another consequence of consuming excessive amounts of animal protein. It is now acknowledged that animal protein fragments can pass through the intestinal lining and make it into the blood stream and thus into the body's circulatory system. When this occurs, it can provoke a response by the body's defenses which are alerted to something "foreign" in the system. The body creates antibodies to attack and destroy the invading protein. Unfortunately, when the antibodies arrive at the scene, they begin to attack everything in sight—including the body's own healthy tissues. The result is autoimmune disease. Rheumatoid arthritis, kidney and arterial inflammations, and insulin-dependent diabetes are examples of the body's defenses going awry due to animal protein in the circulatory system.

Studies show that a plant-based diet—naturally free of all animal protein—can be therapeutic in autoimmune disease. Plant protein does not provoke an attack by the body's defenses. Plant protein is not seen as an invader.

Calcium

Calcium requirements vary by age, gender, and condition. The RDA for calcium approximate 1000 mg. for men, and 1300 mg. for women. On the other hand, the World Health Organization recommends only about one-third those amounts each day. But, how would a recommendation for so little calcium be adequate for bone development and other important bodily functions?

The answer is that in the U.S., virtually all calculations for official calcium recommendations are based on the U.S. and other advanced nations' dietary habits. Namely, meat-based diets are the context in which calcium needs are determined. It has long been known that one of the bodily effects of consuming meat is the loss of calcium. After a meal of animal protein—such as chicken, beef, fish, eggs, and even dairy products—a large amount of amino acids enter the blood, making it acidic. The body neutralizes the acid by taking calcium from your own bones and sending it into the bloodstream. The calcium is then permanently lost as the body sends it out in the urine.

Therefore, societies that eat significant amounts of animal protein lose lots of calcium and so the recommendations are set very high to try to stem the loss. But, it doesn't work. The excessive intake of animal protein drains calcium from the bones no matter how high the official calcium recommendations or calcium dietary intake. The ever-increasing rates of osteoporosis in Western nations bear this out. But, what about drinking lots of milk? The massive Harvard Nurses Health Study, conducted in the late 20th century, found that those nurses who drank 3 or more glasses of milk each day remarkably had higher bone fracture rates than did the non-milk drinkers. Clearly, this study demonstrated that drinking lots of milk provides no protection from bone fractures.

The question must be asked that if milk supposedly is essential for combatting osteoporosis, why are the rates of osteoporosis highest in those countries where the most dairy is consumed, and lowest in nations where little, if any, dairy is consumed?

Scientific evidence makes the indisputable case that the maintenance of strong, healthy bones and the avoidance of osteoporosis depends to a significant degree, not on the amount of calcium you consume, but on the prevention of calcium loss from your bones. The less animal protein you consume, the less calcium is lost. And consuming a wide variety of plant foods, especially the calcium-rich ones, will guarantee the maximum absorption of calcium. The bones are a dynamic organ that can be made stronger by these changes and by adding weight-bearing exercise such as walking and climbing stairs to your daily life.

As far as calcium goes, cow's milk is definitely a source—though plant foods are as good or better a source than milk regarding calcium absorption. But there are many reasons for avoiding milk and other dairy products. Lactose (milk sugar) breaks down in the body to form galactose. When the body is unable to get rid of excess galactose, there is an increased risk of ovarian cancer and infertility.

Dairy products contain saturated fat and cholesterol, contributing to cardiovascular disease—a major killer in Western nations. Low-fat milk is no better—with less fat, the proportion of protein increases. This results in increased blood acidity and to greater calcium loss.

To increase milk production, cows are exposed to growth hormones. These hormones lead to increased reproductive and udder infections in cows and require antibiotic treatment. The resultant milk contains traces of growth hormones, antibiotics, and pus from inflamed udders. The long term health consequences of these adulterants are not known.

It is known, however, that dairy proteins (such as casein) can provoke such allergic and inflammatory reactions in people as: inflammation of joints, skin, and bowels; ear and bronchial infections; asthma; eczema; as well as autoimmune diseases (where the body's white blood cells mistakenly attack the body's own healthy tissues).

There is no scientific evidence that consuming dairy products is required for strong bones. Mounting evidence, instead, points to the need for plant-based calcium since it is more easily absorbed.

Plants are great sources of calcium, especially dark green vegetables such as broccoli, kale, and collard greens. The chart on the next page lists many calcium-rich foods. Not listed are chard, spinach and un-hulled sesame seeds. Each contains oxalates, substances that bind up calcium, making this important mineral only partially absorbable.

Iron

Iron plays an important role in making hemoglobin—the red pigment in blood cells that carries oxygen throughout the body. A deficiency of iron—which affects many younger and pregnant wom-en—means less oxygen is getting to tissues and organs and could lead to anemia, fatigue, headaches, dizziness, lowered immunity, lack of energy, brittle nails, loss of appetite, and other symptoms.

The daily recommended amounts of iron are 10-15 mg. for pre-menopausal women and 8 mg. for adult men and post-menopausal women. The best way to get that iron is to eat a wide variety of plant foods—especially those rich in iron.

Your body is able to regulate carefully the amount of iron it needs to absorb from plant foods. But it cannot control how much iron floods into the bloodstream after eating meat. Heme iron—the iron found in meat—defies your body's control mechanisms and barges in even when your body has adequate iron in storage, as most men and post-menopausal women have. This leads to an iron overload in the blood which can increase the risk of cancer and heart disease. Excess iron also speeds up the production of free radicals—dangerous unstable molecules that damage cells and make cholesterol stick to arte-rial walls. On the other hand, the iron from plant foods does not lead to excess iron in the blood because your body takes in only as much of that iron as it needs.

Many plant foods are iron-rich, and consuming foods high in vita-min C along with those plant foods significantly boosts the amount of iron available to the body. Foods high in vitamin C include citrus, ber-ries, tomatoes, bell peppers, dark leafy greens, cabbage, cauliflower, and broccoli, to mention a few.

Protein, Calcium, & Iron in Selected Foods

	amount	protein (g)	calcium (mg)	iron (mg)
LEGUMES				
black beans, cooked	½ cup	8	60-70	3-4
great northern, cooked	½ cup	7	70-80	3
lentils, cooked	½ cup	8-9	20	3-4
navy beans, cooked	½ cup	8	70-80	3-4
soybeans, cooked	½ cup	14	70-80	3-5
tempeh	4 oz.	20-25	120	3
tofu (firm)	4 oz.	12-20	60-80	2-3
GRAINS				
bread (whole-grain)	1 slice	3	15-25	½-1
brown rice, cooked	1 cup	6	25	1½-2
buckwheat, cooked	1 cup	7	75	2
millet, cooked	1 cup	3	15	3-4
pasta (wh. grain), cooked	1 cup	8-10	10-20	1½-2
quinoa, cooked	1 cup	10-12	85	5-7
rolled oats, cooked	1 cup	5	25	1½-2
VEGETABLES				
broccoli, cooked	1 cup	5-6	180	2
cabbage, cooked	1 cup	2-3	65	½
carrot, raw/cooked	1 medium	1	25-30	½
collard greens, cooked	1 cup	5-7	250-300	2
kale, cooked	1 cup	5	220-250	2-2½
potato, cooked	1 medium	3-4	15-20	3
FRUITS				
banana	1 medium	1-2	10	1
fig	1 medium	½	20-30	½
most fruits	1 medium	1	10-20	½
orange	1 medium	1½-2	60	½
OTHER				
almond butter	1 tablespoon	4	30-40	½-1
almonds	2 tablespoons	3-4	50	½
blackstrap molasses	1 tablespoon	0	100-140	2-3
flax seed meal	2 tablespoons	3	20-30	½-1
peanut butter	1 tablespoon	4	10-15	¼
pumpkin seeds	2 tablespoons	5	10	2
soymilk	1 cup	7-8	50	1-2
soy yogurt	8 oz.	7-9	20-25	1-2
sunflower seeds	2 tablespoons	4-5	20-25	1-2

No-Hassle Cooking with Steam

Cooking with steam results not only in more delicate and flavorful vegetables, but minimizes the loss of valuable water-soluble vitamins and minerals. And it's fast and the clean-up is minimal. The steamer basket is also handy for reheating cooked grains and softening dried fruit. It's also quick and easy to cook tofu and tempeh in the steamer.

Steaming is a method of cooking over, instead of in, boiling water. There's really nothing to it. Fill a pot with about ¾" of water and bring to a boil. Meanwhile, cut your vegetables into uniform size pieces and place in a steamer basket. Place the basket in the pot of boiling water. Cover, lower the heat to maintain just a steady boil, and steam until the veggies are as tender as you like—often, in just a matter of minutes.

When using several vegetables, start steaming the longer-cooking ones (i.e. collards, onions, sweet potatoes, carrots, cauliflower, cabbage, etc.) first for 3-5 minutes, before adding the shorter-cooking ones (i.e. kale, zucchini, broccoli, bell peppers, mushrooms, eggplant, etc.) for the last 2-4 minutes.

While the vegetables are being steamed, the boiling water should not be touching the food. A space between the steamer basket and the boiling water allows steam to circulate around the food.

When your steamed vegetables are tender, toss them in a bowl with a little olive, flax seed, or coconut oil and salt. Or, splash with fresh lemon juice or soy sauce. Then, sprinkle with toasted sesame seeds and chopped fresh herbs, if desired.

If you're new to steaming, start out with an inexpensive **expandable steamer basket** (a compact, stainless-steel basket that opens out like flower petals), before progressing to a **steamer insert** (a stainless-steel, perforated basket that "sits" in a pot well above the boiling water). Finally, there's the **3-piece steamer** (3-tiered stainless-steel baskets), to round out your adventures in steaming.

Basic Beans

Canned beans don't come close to the full, fresh flavor and firm texture of home-cooked beans.

1 cup dried beans (i.e. navy, pinto, lima, garbanzo, kidney, or black beans)

6 cups water (for soaking)

6 cups water (for cooking)

1. Pick through beans, discarding any foreign matter. Rinse beans.
2. Combine beans and 6 cups water in large bowl. Cover and soak overnight (or at least 8 hours) in cool spot or in refrigerator.
3. Drain and rinse soaked beans.
4. Combine soaked beans with 6 cups water in large pot. Bring to boil, reduce heat, cover, and simmer until beans are tender. Check for tenderness after 30-45 minutes for navy, pinto, and black beans. Check after 45-60 minutes for garbanzo and kidney beans.
5. Drain beans. Serve now (see seasonings below) or use in another recipe.

Note: Refrigerate leftovers and use within 5 days or freeze.

Yield: 3-6 servings (2½-3 cups)

Variation: If overnight bean soaking is not possible, use quick-soak method instead. Place dried beans and water in large pot. Bring to boil, then remove from heat for 1-2 hours. Discard soaking water and replace with same amount of fresh water and cook as above.

How to Enjoy Cooked Beans (& Lentils)

- Top with flax seed oil, olive oil, toasted sesame oil, salt, and herbs.
- Toss with hot or cold pasta or grains.
- Add to salads or cooked vegetables.

Basic Red Lentils

These tasty, creamy red legumes are ready in no time! Great with any savory topping. Or, whip up some incredible Red Lentil Dal (page 108).

1 cup dried red lentils

1½ cups water

1. Pick through lentils, discarding any foreign matter. Rinse lentils.
2. Combine water and lentils in large pot. Bring to boil over medium-high heat, reduce heat, cover and simmer 15 minutes.
3. Remove lentils from heat and stir after 5 minutes.
Note: Refrigerate leftovers and use within 5 days or freeze.
Yield: 2-4 servings (about 2 cups)

Basic Brown Lentils

Earthy and peppery, these legumes make hearty side dishes and partners for cooked grains and salads. And try them in 'Cheesy' Lentil Dip (page 82).

1 cup dried brown lentils

3 cups water

1. Pick through lentils, discarding any foreign matter. Rinse lentils.
2. Combine water and lentils in large pot. Bring to boil over medium-high heat, reduce heat, cover and simmer 40 minutes.
3. Remove lentils from heat and drain any remaining cooking liquid.
Note: Refrigerate leftovers and use within 5 days or freeze.
Yield: 4-6 servings (about 3½ cups)

When **cooking legumes** (beans, peas, or lentils) make sure the water and legumes together do not rise above the ¾ level of the cooking pot (to avoid boiling over). Also, when first bringing the legumes to a boil, skim off any foam that forms before covering the pot.

Basic Brown Rice

Slightly nutty and pleasantly chewy, cooked brown rice is welcome at any meal—whether seasoned with sweet or savory seasonings.

1¼ cups uncooked brown rice (long or short-grain)

2 cups water

1. Pick through rice, discarding any foreign matter. Rinse rice.
2. Place rice and water in pot. Bring to boil, reduce heat, cover, and simmer 40 minutes, or until all water is absorbed. Let stand 5-10 minutes, before fluffing with a fork and serving.

Note: Refrigerate leftovers and use within 5 days or freeze.

Yield: 4-8 servings (about 4 cups)

Basic Millet

When cooked with ample water, millet reveals a soft texture and mild nutty flavor. Great as a cereal or in Chocolate Millet Pudding (page 139).

1 cup uncooked millet

3 cups water

1. Pick through millet, discarding any foreign matter. Rinse millet.
2. Place millet and water in pot. Bring to boil, reduce heat, cover, and simmer 20 minutes, or until all water is absorbed. Let stand 5-10 minutes, before fluffing with a fork and serving.

Note: Refrigerate leftovers and use within 5 days or freeze.

Yield: 5-10 servings (about 5 cups)

Variation: For **Millet Porridge**, increase amount of water to 4 cups, and simmer 30 minutes.

For **Millet-Quinoa Porridge**, replace ½ cup uncooked millet with ½ cup uncooked quinoa, increase amount of water to 4 cups, and simmer 30 minutes.

For **Millet-Amaranth Porridge**, replace ½ cup uncooked millet with ½ cup uncooked amaranth, and simmer 30 minutes, stirring frequently during last 15 minutes.

For **Basic Millet & Quinoa**, replace ½ cup uncooked millet with ½ cup uncooked quinoa, decrease amount of water to 2 cups, and simmer 20 minutes.

Basic Quinoa

A mild-tasting high-protein grain that cooks up light and fluffy—
making it a tasty side dish and delightful Tabbouleh (page 60).

1¼ cups uncooked quinoa

2 cups water

1. Pick through quinoa, discarding any foreign matter. Rinse quinoa.
2. Place grains and water in large pot. Bring to boil, reduce heat, cover, and simmer 15 minutes, or until all water is absorbed. Let stand 5-10 minutes, before fluffing with a fork and serving.

Note: Refrigerate leftovers and use within 5 days or freeze.

Yield: 4-8 servings (about 4 cups)

Variation: For a light, fluffy and distinct quinoa, reduce water to 1¼ cups, and simmer 10 minutes, or until all water is absorbed.

Basic Buckwheat

Cooked raw buckwheat has a mild flavor, and moist, fluffy texture.
Serve as a side dish or use in Buckwheat & Bow Ties (page 50).

1¼ cups uncooked raw buckwheat

2 cups water

1. Pick through grains, discarding any foreign matter. Rinse grains.
2. Place grains and water in large pot. Bring to boil, reduce heat, cover, and simmer 15 minutes, or until all water is absorbed. Let stand 5-10 minutes, before fluffing with a fork and serving.

Note: Refrigerate leftovers and use within 5 days or freeze.

Yield: 4-8 servings (about 4 cups)

Variation: For a light, fluffy and distinct buckwheat, reduce water to 1¼ cups, and simmer 10 minutes, or until all water is absorbed.

Seasonings for Cooked Grains

- Garnish with chopped dried or fresh fruit, or nuts and seeds.
- Sprinkle with grated 'Mozzarella Bean Cheese'.
- Top with flax seed oil, olive oil, toasted sesame oil, salt, and herbs.
- Top with Tofu 'Sour Cream', Tofu 'Aioli', or Tangy Black Beans.
- Top with maple syrup, agave nectar, or non-dairy milk.

4-Grain Fusion

Soaking grains overnight shortens cooking time and insures a tender, toothsome combination.

¼ cup each uncooked: long-grain brown rice, wild rice, quinoa, and millet

1¾ cups water

1. Pick through grains, discarding any foreign matter. Rinse.
2. Place grains in bowl with water. Cover and soak overnight (at least 8 hours) in cool spot or in refrigerator.
3. Transfer grains, along with soak water, to pot. Bring to boil, reduce heat, cover, and simmer 25 minutes, or until all water is absorbed. Set aside 5 minutes, then fluff with fork.
Note: Refrigerate leftovers and use within 5 days or freeze.
Yield: 6-11 servings (about 5½ cups)

Sure-Thing Grain Cooking

Here's a cooking method for those who have had no success cooking grains the "usual" way. These grains are cooked in lots of water in an open pot. The result is light, fluffy, and distinct grains.

1 cup uncooked whole grains (select from chart below)

6 cups water
½ teaspoon salt

1. Pick through grains, discarding any foreign matter. Rinse grains.
2. Place grains, water, and salt in pot. Bring to boil, reduce heat, and cook uncovered, for the time shown below.
3. Pour cooked grains in strainer over sink. Then, set strainer over a bowl for 10 minutes to drain. Fluff grains and serve.
Note: Keep pot at steady simmer while cooking and do not stir grains while cooking. This method does not work with buckwheat.
Refrigerate leftovers and use within 5 days or freeze.
Yield: 4-8 servings (about 4 cups)

Grains:	Cooking Times:
quinoa	15 minutes
millet	20 minutes
brown rice	40 minutes
wild rice	60 minutes

Homemade Oat Flour

Homemade oat flour reveals a sweet flavor and coarse meal.
Try it in Apple Bread (page 143) or Orange Bean Cake (page 147).

3 cups rolled oats

1. Place 1½ cups oats in blender and grind into flour.
2. Remove flour from blender and grind remaining oats.
Note: Store leftover flour in airtight container in refrigerator and use within 60 days or freeze.
Yield: about 2½ cups
Variation: Replace rolled oats with uncooked whole oats (also called oat groats). Place 1¼ cups whole oats at a time in blender and grind into flour.

Homemade Millet Flour

This homemade flour is both coarser and fresher than store-bought.
It's great in Millet Cornbread (page 146).

2½ cups uncooked millet

1. Pick through millet, discarding any foreign matter.
2. Place 1¼ cups millet in blender and grind into flour.
3. Remove flour from blender and grind remaining millet.
Note: Store leftover flour in airtight container in refrigerator and use within 60 days or freeze.
Yield: about 2 cups
Variation: For **Homemade Buckwheat Flour**, replace millet with uncooked, raw buckwheat. Place 1¼ cups buckwheat at a time in blender and grind into flour.

Cooking extra is a great way to save time in the kitchen. When cooking beans, grains, or other dishes, double (or even triple!) recipes and freeze half for meals at a later date.

Flax Seed Meal

This makes a tasty and highly-nutritious addition to cereals, smoothies, soy yogurt, and quickbreads of all kinds.

1 cup flax seeds

1. Place up to ¼ cup flax seeds in small electric spice or coffee grinder and grind into coarse powder. Or, place ⅓ cup flax seeds in blender and grind into coarse powder.
2. Continue with remaining flax seeds.
Note: Store leftover flax meal in airtight container in freezer and use within 45 days.
Yield: about 1½ cups

Basic Dough & 'Sourdough'

From this one simple dough, a variety of exceptional quickbreads shall a-rise! These include bagels, scones, rolls, pizza crust, and sticky buns.

1 cup each: brown rice flour and oat flour (see note)
¼ cup flax seed meal (see recipe above)
2 teaspoons baking powder (aluminum-free)
½ teaspoon salt

1 cup non-dairy milk
3 tablespoons cashew butter or almond butter

1. Combine first 4 dry ingredients in bowl.
2. In small bowl, whisk next 2 wet ingredients.
3. Transfer wet ingredients to bowl of dry ingredients and mix well until dough holds together and a dough ball can be formed.
5. Place dough ball on floured surface and knead briefly, adding more rice or oat flour as necessary to form soft, pliable, non-sticky ball. Return ball to bowl and let rest 5 minutes. Dough is ready for use in other recipes.
Note: Store-bought oat flour is recommended as it's finer than homemade oat flour and will yield a more delicate texture.
Variation: Replace oat flour with whole-grain sorghum flour, and increase non-dairy milk to 1¼ cups.

For **Basic 'Sourdough'**, replace ⅓ cup non-dairy milk with ⅓ cup fresh lemon juice.

Roasted Nuts

Roasted nuts provide a distinctive flavor and appealing crunchy texture to many dishes. Tofu 'Egg Fried' Rice (page 128) immediately comes to mind.

1 cup raw almonds, walnuts or other nuts (shelled)

salt (to taste) (optional)

1. Preheat oven to 325°.
2. Pick through nuts, discarding any foreign matter.
3. Rinse nuts in strainer and shake to remove moisture.
4. Spread nuts on un-oiled baking sheet. Sprinkle with salt, if using. Bake 5 minutes, stir, and bake 5 minutes more, or until golden.
5. Tranfer hot nuts to plate to cool.

Note: Store cooled leftovers in airtight container in refrigerator or freezer and use within 60 days.

Yield: about 1 cup

Roasted Seeds

A light roasting brings out a rich flavor and crunchy texture. Roasted seeds make a sensational topping for salads, pasta, grains, and stir-fries.

1 cup raw sunflower, sesame, or other seeds

salt (to taste) (optional)

1. Preheat oven to 325°.
2. Pick through seeds, discarding any foreign matter.
3. Rinse seeds in fine-mesh strainer and shake to remove moisture.
4. Spread seeds on un-oiled baking sheet. Sprinkle with salt, if using. Bake 5 minutes, stir, and bake 3 minutes more, or until golden.
5. Tranfer hot seeds to plate to cool.

Note: Store cooled leftovers in airtight container in refrigerator or freezer and use within 60 days.

Yield: about 1 cup

Variation: For **Roasted Sunflower Seed Meal**, place roasted sunflower seeds in blender and grind into coarse powder or meal (about 15 seconds). Store leftover seed meal in airtight container in refrigerator or freezer and use within 45 days.

2 Beverages

Almond Milk

With its delicate, nutty flavor and creamy white complexion, this almond milk makes an ideal replacement for dairy milk.

¾ cup raw almonds
3 cups water (for soaking)

3 cups water (for blending)

1 tablespoon maple syrup or agave nectar
½ teaspoon vanilla extract
¼ teaspoon salt

1. Pick through nuts and discard any foreign matter. Rinse nuts.
2. Place water and nuts in a bowl, cover and refrigerate 4-8 hours.
3. Drain and rinse soaked nuts. Blend nuts with 1 cup water until smooth. With blender on, pour remaining 2 cups water through opening in blender top and blend for 30 seconds.
4. Pour blender mixture through fine-meshed strainer (or in strainer lined with dampened, unbleached cheesecloth for ultra-smooth milk) over bowl. Press milk against strainer with back of large spoon to push liquid through.
5. Return milk to blender with remaining seasonings and blend.
Note: Remaining nut pulp can be added in small amounts (i.e. ½ cup per recipe) to quickbread, muffin, or cookie recipes.
Refrigerate leftovers in glass jar and use within 5 days.
Yield: about 3 cups
Variation: Replace almonds with other nuts (i.e. pecans, cashews, or filberts).

Instant Nut Milk

Need milk in a hurry? Here's a quick and easy way to get it.

2 cups water
3-4 tablespoons almond, cashew, or other nut or seed butter
½ teaspoon vanilla extract
pinch of salt

1. Place all ingredients in blender and blend until smooth.
Note: Refrigerate leftovers in glass jar and use within 5 days.
Yield: about 2¼ cups

Rice Milk

Want rice milk? All you need is cooked brown rice and a blender.

1 cup cooked long-grain brown rice (page 25)
2 cups water

1 tablespoon maple syrup or agave nectar
2 teaspoons canola oil
½ teaspoon vanilla extract
pinch of salt

    1. Place cooked rice in blender with 1 cup water and blend until smooth. With blender running, pour remaining 1 cup water through opening in blender top and continue blending 30 seconds.

    2. Pour blender mixture through fine-meshed strainer (or in strainer lined with dampened, unbleached cheesecloth for ultra-smooth milk) over bowl. Press milk against strainer with back of large spoon to push liquid through.

    3. Return milk to blender with remaining seasonings and blend.

Note: Refrigerate leftovers in glass jar and use within 5 days.

Yield: about 2 cups

Oat Milk

This rich-tasting milk has an enticing oat flavor.

3 cups water
1¼ cups rolled oats

2 tablespoons maple syrup or agave nectar
1 tablespoon canola oil
1 teaspoon vanilla extract
¼ teaspoon salt

    1. Place water and oats in bowl, cover and refrigerate at least 2 hours.

    2. Transfer oat mixture to blender and blend 60 seconds.

    3. Pour blender mixture through fine-meshed strainer (or in strainer lined with dampened, unbleached cheesecloth for ultra-smooth milk) over bowl. Press milk against strainer with back of large spoon to push liquid through.

    4. Return milk to blender with remaining seasonings and blend.

Note: Refrigerate leftovers in glass jar and use within 5 days.

Yield: about 2¾ cups

Soy Milk

Turning soybeans into milk is truly a wonder.
This recipe, of twice boiling the beans, yields a tasty milk.

¾ cup dried soybeans
4 cups water (for soaking)

5 cups water (for cooking)

5 cups water (for cooking)

3½ cups water (for blending)

2 tablespoons maple syrup or agave nectar
1 teaspoon vanilla extract
¼ teaspoon salt

1. Pick through beans, discarding any foreign matter. Rinse beans.
2. Place beans and 4 cups water in bowl, cover and refrigerate at least 8 hours.
3. Drain and rinse soaked beans.
4. Place soaked beans in pot with 5 cups water. Bring to boil, reduce heat, cover, and simmer 10 minutes.
5. Drain and rinse boiled beans. Place boiled beans in pot with 5 cups water. Again, bring to boil, reduce heat, cover, and simmer 10 minutes.
6. Drain and rinse beans.
7. Place beans in blender and blend with 1 cup water until smooth. With blender running, pour remaining 2½ cups water through opening in blender top and continue blending 30 seconds.
8. Pour blender mixture through fine-meshed strainer (or in strainer lined with dampened, unbleached cheesecloth for ultra-smooth milk) over bowl. Press milk against strainer with back of large spoon to push liquid through.
9. Return milk to blender with remaining seasonings and blend.
Note: Refrigerate leftovers in glass jar and use within 5 days.
Yield: about 3 cups

A beverage like **ginger tea** not only refreshes, but may help relieve cold symptoms, intestinal distress, and pain from inflamed joints. Simply place a 1" piece of fresh ginger (sliced) in a cup of boiling water. Sweeten, if desired.

Coconut Milk

*A rich, velvety-smooth milk that's fresher and tastier
than any commercially prepared coconut milk.*

2¼ cups boiling water
1½ cups dried, unsweetened shredded coconut

1. Combine boiling water and coconut in glass bowl. Stir mixture, cover, and let stand until cool, about 45 minutes.
2. Transfer mixture to blender and blend 1 minute.
3. Pour blender mixture through fine-meshed strainer (or in strainer lined with dampened, unbleached cheesecloth for ultra-smooth milk) over bowl. Press milk against strainer with back of large spoon to push liquid through.
Note: Remaining coconut pulp can be added in small amounts (i.e. ½ cup per recipe) to quickbread, muffin, or cookie recipes.
Refrigerate leftovers in glass jar and use within 5 days.
Yield: about 1½ cups
Variation: For thinner, less-rich milk, increase water to 3 or 4 cups.

'Piña Coladas'

*A classic tropical drink that combines the flavors of coconut and pineapple.
Thick, luscious, and radiant—even without the rum.*

1¼ cups Coconut Milk (see recipe above)
¼ cup frozen pineapple juice concentrate
1 frozen banana (chopped)
1 cup frozen strawberries
1 tablespoon maple syrup or agave nectar
1 teaspoon vanilla extract
pinch of salt

1. Place all ingredients in blender and blend until smooth.
Note: For thinner drink, increase coconut milk by ¼ cup.
Yield: about 3 cups

With **frozen bananas** on hand, you've got the makings for shakes, 'Piña Coladas', and 'Lassis'. Simply peel ripe bananas and place them in an airtight container in your freezer overnight. Frozen bananas will last 2-3 weeks in your freezer.

Chocolate Milk

Chocolate milk really takes off when using fresh, homemade milk.

2 cups non-dairy milk
2 tablespoons cocoa powder
2 tablespoons sugar (i.e. evaporated cane juice)
1 tablespoon peanut butter or other nut butter
½ teaspoon vanilla extract
pinch of salt

1. Place all ingredients in blender and blend until smooth.
Note: Refrigerate leftovers in glass jar and use within 5 days.
Yield: about 2 cups
Variation: For **Hot Chocolate,** blend 2 tablespoons non-dairy chocolate chips with all ingredients until smooth. Pour blender mixture into pot and bring to slow simmer on medium heat, stirring frequently. Stir in a mixture of 2 tablespoons arrowroot powder dissolved in 2 tablespoons cold water into simmering chocolate milk and continue stirring until milk thickens.

Oat 'Cream'

Whole oats yield their hidden richness in this creamy, smooth topping.
Enjoy it over fresh fruit, porridge, or cobbler.

1 cup whole oats (also called oat groats)
3 cups water (for soaking)

1½ cups water (for blending)

2 tablespoons maple syrup or agave nectar
½ teaspoon vanilla extract
¼ teaspoon salt

1. Place oats and 3 cups water in bowl, cover and refrigerate 24-36 hours.
2. Drain and rinse oats. Blend oats with ½ cup water or until smooth. With blender running, pour remaining 1 cup water through opening in blender top and continue blending 30 seconds.
3. Pour blender mixture through fine-meshed strainer over bowl. Press cream against strainer with spoon to push liquid through.
4. Return cream to blender with remaining seasonings and blend.
Note: Refrigerate leftovers in glass jar and use within 5 days.
Yield: about 1½ cups

Great Shakes

These remarkably great shakes burst with flavor and nourishment.

Chocolate Shake

1 cup non-dairy milk
6 ice cubes
1½ frozen bananas (chopped)
2 tablespoons cocoa powder
2 tablespoons sugar (i.e. evaporated cane juice)
1 tablespoon peanut butter or other nut butter
1 tablespoon non-dairy chocolate chips (optional)
1 teaspoon vanilla extract
pinch of salt

1. Place all ingredients in blender and blend until smooth.
Yield: 1-2 servings

Vanilla Shake

1 cup non-dairy milk
6 ice cubes
1½ frozen bananas (chopped)
2 tablespoons maple syrup or agave nectar
1 tablespoon almond butter or cashew butter
1½ teaspoons vanilla extract
pinch of salt

1. Place all ingredients in blender and blend until smooth.
Yield: 1-2 servings

Blueberry Shake

1½ cups non-dairy milk
6 ice cubes
3 large dates (chopped) (optional)
1½ cups frozen blueberries (or other berries)
1½ frozen bananas (chopped)
3 tablespoons maple syrup or agave nectar
1 teaspoon vanilla extract
pinch of salt

1. Place all ingredients in blender and blend until smooth.
Yield: 2 servings

Oat Raisin Smoothie

No time for a leisurely breakfast? This wholesome and hearty drinkable meal is just the thing when you only have time to grab-and-go.

1¼ cups non-dairy milk
¼ cup rolled oats
3 tablespoons raisins or other dried fruit (chopped)
1 tablespoon flax seed meal (page 29)

½ cup soy or other non-dairy yogurt (plain or flavored)
1 tablespoon almond, cashew, or other nut butter
¼ teaspoon vanilla extract
pinch of each: cinnamon and salt

1. Place first 4 ingredients in bowl, cover and refrigerate 4-8 hours.
2. Pour oat mixture into blender with remaining ingredients. Blend until smooth.

Note: Refrigerate leftovers in glass jar and use within 5 days.

Smoothie will thicken as it chills in refrigerator. Stir in a little non-dairy milk to thin, if desired.

Yield: 1-2 servings

Variation: For **Rice Date Smoothie**, replace oats with ¾ cup cooked brown rice (page 25) and replace raisins with 3 tablespoons chopped dates.

'Horchata'

*Popular in Mexico and Spain, horchatas are lightly-sweetened drinks
made by blending soaked nuts and grains. Remarkably good.*

¾ cup uncooked long-grain brown rice
½ cup raw almonds
2 cups water (for soaking)

3 cups water (for blending)

2 tablespoons maple syrup or agave nectar
1 teaspoon vanilla extract
¼ teaspoon salt

1. Pick through rice and almonds, discarding any foreign matter.
Rinse rice and almonds.
2. Place rice, almonds, and 2 cups water in bowl, cover and
refrigerate 18-24 hours.
3. Drain and rinse rice and almonds. Blend with 1 cup water until
smooth. With blender running, pour remaining 2 cups water through
opening in blender top and continue blending for 30 seconds.
4. Pour blender mixture through fine-meshed strainer (or in strainer
lined with dampened, unbleached cheesecloth for ultra-smooth milk)
over bowl. Press milk against strainer with back of large spoon to
push liquid through.
5. Return milk to blender with remaining seasonings and blend.
Note: Refrigerate leftovers in glass jar and use within 5 days.
Yield: 2-3 servings

'Margaritas'

*Served in tall, iced glasses, these frosty,
tequila-free "margaritas" are extraordinarily flavorful.*

½ cup water
¼ cup frozen orange juice concentrate
¼ cup each: fresh lemon juice and fresh lime juice
2 tablespoons maple syrup or agave nectar
8 ice cubes

1. Place all ingredients in blender and blend until smooth.
Yield: 2-3 servings

'Buttermilk'

Creamy and tart, homemade buttermilk is a fresh, cholesterol-free departure from "the real thing." Use it everywhere buttermilk is called for.

1¾ cups Almond Milk (page 32)
¼ cup fresh lemon juice
pinch of salt

1. Combine all ingredients in bowl and mix thoroughly.
Note: Refrigerate leftovers in glass jar and use within 5 days.
Yield: 2 cups

Cucumber 'Lassi'

Cooling buttermilk drinks called 'lassis' are the rage in India.
This one combines a tangy flavor with that of earthy cucumber. Invigorating!

3 cups cucumbers (peeled and seeded, if desired, and chopped)
2 cups 'Buttermilk' (see recipe above)
¼ teaspoon salt

1. Place all ingredients in blender and blend until smooth.
Note: Serve chilled, with or without ice cubes or crushed ice.
Refrigerate leftovers in glass jar and use within 2 days.
Yield: 2-3 servings

Banana-Strawberry 'Lassi'

A popular, buttermilk drink in South Asia,
this fruity lassi is especially good over crushed ice.

2 cups 'Buttermilk' (see recipe above)
2 frozen bananas (chopped)
2 cups frozen strawberries
2 tablespoons maple syrup or agave nectar
1 teaspoon vanilla extract
pinch of salt

1. Place all ingredients in blender and blend until smooth.
Note: Serve with or without ice cubes or crushed ice.
Yield: 2-3 servings

3 Grains, Cereals, & Noodles

Kasha Krunch Cereal

A tasty cereal that's crunchy, chewy, nutty—and most of all—addictive!

3 cups uncooked raw buckwheat

½ cup almonds, pecans, or other nuts (chopped)
½ cup sugar (i.e. evaporated cane juice)
1 tablespoon coconut oil (melted) or canola oil
½ teaspoon each: cinnamon and salt

¾ cup raisins or other dried fruit (chopped)
3 tablespoons peanut butter or other seed or nut butter

1. Preheat oven to 300°.
2. Pick through grains, discarding any foreign matter. Rinse grains.
3. In bowl, mix buckwheat with next 5 ingredients.
4. Spread mixture on large, oiled baking sheet (or baking dish).
5. Bake 20 minutes. Stir and bake 20 minutes more.
6. Transfer hot grains to bowl. Mix with raisins and peanut butter.

Note: Refrigerate leftovers and use within 14 days.
Yield: 6-8 servings

Tofu French Toast

Crisp-baked French toast. Extraordinary topped with chopped nuts (page 30).

4 ounces firm tofu
1 cup non-dairy milk
1 tablespoon sugar (i.e. evaporated cane juice)
½ teaspoon each: cinnamon, salt, and vanilla extract
pinch of ground turmeric

6 slices whole-grain bread

1 recipe Cinnamon Maple Glaze (optional) (page 151)

1. Preheat oven to 350°.
2. In blender, blend first 7 ingredients until smooth.
3. Place bread in single layer in shallow dish. Pour blender mixture over bread, turning to saturate both sides.
4. Transfer soaked bread to oiled baking sheet and bake 15 minutes. Turn slices over and bake 15 minutes longer, or until golden brown.
5. Top with glaze and serve.

Note: Refrigerate leftovers and use within 5 days.
Yield: 3-6 servings

Flax-Date Granola

A remarkably tasty and healthy homemade granola.

2½ cups rolled oats
½ cup almonds, pecans, or other nuts (chopped)
½ cup dried, unsweetened shredded coconut
¼ cup flax seed meal (page 29)
1 teaspoon cinnamon
½ teaspoon salt

½ cup maple syrup or agave nectar
2 tablespoons coconut oil or canola oil
2 teaspoons vanilla extract

½ cup dried dates (chopped)

1. Preheat oven to 325°.
2. Combine first 6 dry ingredients in large bowl.
3. In pot, briefly warm next 3 wet ingredients.
4. In bowl, combine dry and wet ingredients. Mix well. Stir in dates.
5. Spread mixture on large, oiled baking sheet and bake 25 minutes, stirring halfway.

Note: Refrigerate leftovers and use within 10 days.
Yield: 4-6 servings

Muesli

My delicious mix of oats, fruits, and seeds soaked in liquid overnight recalls a popular breakfast cereal developed in the 19th century Swiss Alps.

1½ cups non-dairy milk
¾ cup rolled oats
1 medium apple (cored and grated or chopped)
¼ cup sunflower seeds or nuts (chopped)
¼ cup raisins or other dried fruit (chopped)
2 tablespoons flax seed meal (page 29)
2 tablespoons maple syrup or agave nectar (optional)
pinch of cinnamon and salt

1. Combine all ingredients in bowl. Cover and refrigerate overnight (or at least 4 hours). Mix well before serving.

Note: Refrigerate leftovers and use within 3 days.
Yield: 2-3 servings

Creamy Oatmeal

Creamy rolled oats simmering with dates in cinnamon-infused "milk."

2 cups non-dairy milk
1 cup rolled oats
½ cup dried dates or other dried fruit (chopped)
½ teaspoon cinnamon
¼ teaspoon salt

3 tablespoons flax seed meal (optional) (page 29)

1. Place all ingredients, except flax meal, in pot. Bring to boil over medium heat, reduce heat, cover, and simmer 5 minutes.
2. Before serving, stir in flax meal, if using.
Note: Refrigerate leftovers and use within 7 days.
Yield: 2 servings
Variation: For **Chocolate Creamy Oatmeal**, before serving, stir in 3 tablespoons cocoa powder, 2 tablespoons maple syrup, and 1 tablespoon nut butter. Sprinkle servings with non-dairy chocolate chips, chopped nuts (page 30), or assorted berries.

Brown Rice Porridge

Garnished with berries and nuts, this delicately sweet and creamy porridge is like having dessert for breakfast.

3 cups cooked brown rice (page 25)
1½ cups non-dairy milk
¼ cup dried dates or other dried fruit (chopped)
2 tablespoons maple syrup or agave nectar
1 teaspoon vanilla extract
¼ teaspoon salt

¼ cup flax seed meal (optional) (page 29)

1 cup berries (fresh or frozen and thawed)
¾ cup walnuts or other nuts (chopped)

1. Combine first 6 ingredients in pot. Bring to simmer over medium heat, stirring occasionally. Reduce heat, cover, and simmer 20 minutes, stirring occasionally.
2. Remove pot from heat, stir in flax meal (if using) and spoon porridge into individual bowls. Top evenly with nuts and berries.
Note: Refrigerate leftovers and use within 4 days.
Yield: 3-4 servings

Banana Flapjacks

Light, fluffy pancakes made from whole rice and oat flours.

¾ cup each: brown rice flour and oat flour (see note)
2 teaspoons baking powder (aluminum-free)
1 teaspoon cinnamon
¼ teaspoon salt

1 cup non-dairy milk
2 medium ripe bananas
2 tablespoons peanut butter or other nut butter
2 tablespoons maple syrup or agave nectar
1 teaspoon vanilla extract

1. Combine first 5 dry ingredients in bowl.
2. In blender, blend next 5 wet ingredients.
3. Pour wet ingredients into bowl of dry ingredients. Mix well, adding a little more milk, if necessary, to thin.
4. Heat oiled, non-stick skillet over medium heat. Skillet is ready when a drop of water "dances" over the surface.
5. For each flapjack, pour ¼ cup batter into skillet. Cook until bubbles form on tops of flapjacks and bottoms are golden brown, 2-3 minutes. Flip and cook other sides until golden, about 1 minute.
6. Serve now, or keep cooked flapjacks warm in 200° oven while remaining flapjacks are prepared.
Note: Store-bought oat flour is much finer than homemade oat flour and will yield more delicate pancakes.
Refrigerate leftovers and use within 4 days.
Yield: 3-4 servings

Flapjack Sandwiches

Yummy fillings pressed between delectable, banana-flavored pancakes.

1 recipe Banana Flapjacks (see recipe above)

Fillings (to taste):
peanut butter or other nut butter, jelly, raisins, roasted nuts or seeds, bananas slices, and shredded coconut

1. Lay flapjacks on flat surface and spread every other one with peanut butter, and then with jelly. Top with remaining ingredients and cover with remaining flapjacks, pressing down, to form sandwiches.
Yield: 3-4 servings

Cornbread

An uncommon cornbread of corn and rice—with a moist,
delicate crumb that's infused with maple sweetness.

1 cup each: cornmeal (unrefined) and brown rice flour
¼ cup flax seed meal (page 29)
2 teaspoons baking powder (aluminum-free)
½ teaspoon salt

1½ cups non-dairy milk
¼ cup maple syrup or agave nectar
3 tablespoons cashew butter or almond butter
2 tablespoons fresh lemon juice

1. Preheat oven to 425°.
2. Combine first 5 dry ingredients in bowl.
3. In small bowl, whisk next 4 ingredients. Mix with dry ingredients.
4. Transfer batter into oiled 8x8" baking pan or into two small loaf pans, and bake 30 minutes, or until golden and firm.
Note: Refrigerate leftovers and use within 5 days.
Yield: 6-8 servings

Brown Rice Risotto

A rich, creamy whole-grain version of a classic Italian dish.

1 cup uncooked short-grain brown rice

4 cups water
3 tablespoons Dry Vegetable Broth Seasoning (page 90)
½ teaspoon salt

4 cups broccoli florets (cut in bite-sized pieces)

Sesame 'Parmesan' (to taste) (page 75)

1. Pick through rice, discarding any foreign matter. Rinse rice.
2. Combine rice, water, broth seasoning, and salt in pot. Bring to boil, reduce heat, cover, and simmer 1¼ hours.
3. Remove rice from heat and let stand 10 minutes. Gently stir.
4. Place broccoli in steamer basket and steam 3 minutes.
5. Stir broccoli into rice and garnish with Sesame 'Parmesan'.
Note: Refrigerate leftovers and use within 3 days.
Yield: 4-6 servings

Rice Garbo Bars

These tasty cake-like bars will leave other protein bars in the dust.

2 cups brown rice flour
¾ cup garbanzo bean flour
¾ cup walnuts, pecans, or other nuts (chopped)
¾ cup raisins or other dried fruit (chopped)
½ cup sugar (i.e. evaporated cane juice)
½ cup non-dairy chocolate chips
¼ cup flax seed meal (page 29)
2 teaspoons each: baking powder and cinnamon
½ teaspoon salt

2½ cups non-dairy milk
2 tablespoons peanut butter or other nut butter
2 teaspoons vanilla extract

1. Preheat oven to 350°.
2. In large bowl, combine first 10 dry ingredients.
3. In small bowl, whisk next 3 ingredients. Mix with dry ingredients.
4. Spread mixture into oiled 9x13" (or similar-sized) baking pan.
5. Bake 35 minutes or until golden. Cool, then cut into bars.
Note: Refrigerate leftovers and use within 5 days or freeze.
Yield: 8-12 servings

Rice-Millet Polenta

This thick, smooth "mush" is delectable with either
a maple glaze (page 151) or a little olive oil and salt.

3¾ cups water

1½ cups non-dairy milk
½ cup each: brown rice flour and millet flour (see note)
½ teaspoon salt

1. Bring water to boil in pot.
2. Combine next 4 ingredients in bowl, mixing well.
3. Pour mixture slowly into boiling water, stirring briskly.
4. Lower heat and simmer polenta, covered, 15 minutes, until thick and creamy, like mashed potatoes. Stir frequently.
Note: Store-bought millet flour is much finer than coarser homemade millet flour and will yield a smoother texture.
Refrigerate leftovers and use within 5 days.
Yield: 4-8 servings

Garbo Rounds

These crisp, tasty crackers are made of brown rice, beans, and seeds.

1 cup each: garbanzo bean flour and brown rice flour
¾ cup roasted sunflower seed meal (page 30)
¼ cup flax seed meal (page 29)
2 teaspoons baking powder (aluminum-free)
2 teaspoons onion powder
1 teaspoon caraway seeds (optional)
¾ teaspoon salt

1 cup water
¼ cup fresh lemon juice

1. Preheat oven to 350°.

2. In bowl, combine first 8 dry ingredients.

3. In separate bowl, combine next 2 wet ingredients. Mix with dry ingredients, adding either more water or rice flour, 1 tablespoon at a time, to form a firm dough ball. Let dough rest 5 minutes.

4. Place dough ball on floured surface and knead briefly, adding more rice flour as necessary to form soft, pliable, non-sticky dough ball. Return dough ball to bowl and let rest 5 minutes.

5. Cut and form dough into 2 dough balls, then roll each into 2 logs, each about 8" in length.

6. Slice dough logs into ½" thick rounds.

7. Transfer rounds to oiled, non-stick baking sheet.

8. Bake 15 minutes. Flip rounds and bake 15 minutes more, or until as golden as desired.

Note: Refrigerate leftovers and use within 5 days or freeze.

Yield: 4-6 servings

An oven rack can double up as a wire or cooling rack. Before turning on your oven, remove the bottom rack and place it on a countertop. Wipe it down, if necessary, and use it for cooling baked goods. When the cooling is over, the oven rack disappears right back into the oven.

'Sourdough' Bagels

These toothsome bagels are crusty outside, soft and chewy inside.

1 recipe Basic 'Sourdough' (page 29)

3 quarts water
2 tablespoons salt or baking soda

salt (to taste)
sesame seeds or poppy seeds (to taste)

1. Preheat oven to 400°.
2. Place dough ball on floured surface. Cut ball in half, then in half again, and continue, until there are 8 equal size balls.
3. Poke hole through each dough ball with finger or small round cookie cutter. Collect cut-outs to make additional bagel.
4. Bring water and salt to boil in large pot.
5. Drop several bagels at a time into boiling water and cook 1 minute, stirring occasionally.
6. Remove bagels with slotted spoon and place on dry plate (for bagels to drain). Sprinkle with salt and seeds, then transfer to oiled, non-stick baking sheet.
7. Bake 15 minutes. Flip bagels and bake 10 minutes more, or until as golden as desired.
Note: Refrigerate leftovers and use within 5 days or freeze.
Yield: 4-6 servings

'Sourdough' Scones

These thick, triangular-shaped scones emerge from the oven crusty and chewy.
Outstanding brushed with a little olive oil and salt or topped with jam.

1 recipe Basic 'Sourdough' (page 29)

1-2 tablespoons non-dairy milk
salt (to taste)

1. Preheat oven to 400°.
2. On floured surface, roll dough into 8" circle, about ¾" thick.
3. Cut into 12 wedges. Transfer to oiled, baking sheet. Brush or dab about ¼ teaspoon milk over each wedge and sprinkle with salt.
4. Bake 22 minutes, or until as crisp and golden as desired.
Note: Refrigerate leftovers and use within 5 days or freeze.
Yield: 4-6 servings

Buckwheat & Bow Ties

An old European dish, ideal topped with Tofu 'Sour Cream' (page 86).

1 cup uncooked raw buckwheat
1 cup water

1 medium onion (chopped)
2 medium garlic cloves (finely chopped)

2 cups uncooked, whole-grain bow tie (or other) noodles

2 tablespoons toasted sesame oil or olive oil
¾ teaspoon salt

1. Pick through buckwheat, discarding any foreign matter. Rinse buckwheat.
2. Combine buckwheat and water in pot. Bring to boil, reduce heat, cover, and simmer 10 minutes or until all water is absorbed. Set aside.
3. In an oiled non-stick skillet, stir-fry onions and garlic over medium heat, uncovered, until onions are tender.
4. Cook noodles in boiling water 8-10 minutes, or until tender. Drain noodles, return to pot, and toss with sesame oil and salt.
5. Transfer cooked noodles and buckwheat to skillet and combine with cooked onions and garlic. Heat thoroughly before serving.
Note: Refrigerate leftovers and use within 5 days.
Yield: 4-6 servings

Raw Buckwheat Cereal

An all-raw cereal made even better topped with fresh fruit!

¼ cup each: uncooked raw buckwheat and raw seeds or nuts
2 cups water

1 cup Almond Milk (page 32)
¼ cup dried fruit (chopped) or raisins
2 tablespoons flax seed meal (page 29)
pinch of cinnamon and salt

1. In bowl, combine first 3 ingredients. Cover and soak overnight (or at least 4 hours) in refrigerator.
2. Rinse soaked buckwheat mixture thoroughly in strainer.
3. Combine in bowl with remaining ingredients.
Yield: 1 serving

Fettuccine Alfredo with Broccoli

Instead of white noodles swimming in a heavy, buttery sauce, my whole-grain noodles are enrobed in a light, nourishing "sour cream."

8 ounces uncooked whole-grain noodles (preferably narrow and flat)

1 tablespoon olive oil or coconut oil (melted)
½ teaspoon salt
pinch of black pepper

4 cups broccoli florets (cut in bite-sized pieces)

1 recipe Tofu 'Sour Cream' (page 86) or Tofu 'Aioli' (page 85)

1. Cook noodles in boiling water 8-10 minutes, or until tender. Drain noodles, return to pot, and toss with oil, salt, and pepper.
2. Place broccoli in steamer basket and steam 3 minutes, or until bright green and just tender.
3. Combine noodles and broccoli and top with sour cream.
Note: Refrigerate leftovers and use within 4 days.
Yield: 3-4 servings

Quinoa & Red Lentil Pilaf

A protein and fiber-rich dish. Earthy, nutty, and very satisfying.

1 cup uncooked quinoa
½ cup dried red lentils

2 cups water
2 tablespoons olive oil or coconut oil
2 teaspoons onion powder
1 teaspoon garlic powder
¾ teaspoon salt

1. Pick through quinoa and lentils, discarding any foreign matter. Rinse quinoa and lentils.
2. Combine all ingredients in pot. Bring to boil over medium heat, reduce heat, cover, and simmer 15 minutes. Let stand 5 minutes. Stir before serving.
Note: Refrigerate leftovers and use within 5 days.
Yield: 4-6 servings

'Pad Thai'

This wholesome version of the popular Thai noodle dish combines vibrant veggies with brown rice noodles and tofu—all bathed in an aromatic sauce.

8 ounces uncooked whole-grain noodles (preferably narrow and flat)

1 tablespoon toasted sesame oil or olive oil
¼ teaspoon salt

1 medium carrot (cut in matchsticks)
1 small turnip or daikon radish (cut in matchsticks)
½ medium red bell pepper (seeded and cut in thin strips)

½ cup green peas (fresh or frozen and thawed)

1 recipe Tofu 'Cutlets' (cut in thin strips) (page 94)
1 recipe Thai Sauce (page 90)

2-4 tablespoons Roasted Sesame Seeds (optional) (page 30)

1. Cook noodles in boiling water 8-10 minutes, or until tender. Drain noodles, return to pot, and toss with oil and salt. Set aside.

2. Place next 3 vegetables in steamer basket and steam 3 minutes. Add peas and steam for 2 minutes more.

3. Transfer steamed vegetables to pot with noodles and combine. Stir in tofu and sauce. Sprinkle with sesame seeds.

Note: Refrigerate leftovers and use within 3 days.
Yield: 3-4 servings

4 Salads & Dressings

Tofu 'Tuna' Salad

Tofu absorbs and combines many distinctive flavors in this delicious tuna-free salad. Enjoy it on a green salad, stuffed in pita, or as a side dish all its own.

16 ounces firm tofu

¾ cup celery (finely chopped)
¾ cup green onions (thinly sliced)
3 tablespoons each: tahini and soy sauce
1½ tablespoons fresh lemon juice
1½ teaspoons onion powder

1. Bring small pot of water to boil. Cut tofu in several pieces, and boil 5 minutes. Rinse tofu under cold water until cool.

2. Place tofu in mixing bowl and mash with fork. Add remaining ingredients and thoroughly combine.

Note: Refrigerate leftovers and use within 7 days.

For serving ideas, see page 83.

Yield: 3-4 servings

Tempeh 'Chicken' Salad

Tempeh and tangy tofu mayo make an exceptional duo.
Toss in crunchy celery and pickles and you've really got a super salad.

8 ounces tempeh (cut in several pieces)

1 cup Tofu 'Mayonnaise' (page 85)
¼ cup celery (finely chopped)
¼ cup green onions (thinly sliced)
2 medium dill pickles (finely chopped)
2 teaspoons Dijon-style or stone-ground mustard
¼ teaspoon salt

1. Place tempeh in steamer basket and steam 15 minutes.

2. Remove tempeh from steamer and let cool to touch.

3. Grate or mash tempeh in mixing bowl. Combine with remaining ingredients.

Note: Refrigerate leftovers and use within 3 days.

For serving ideas, see page 83.

Yield: 3 servings

Tofu 'Egg' Salad

Turmeric lends an egg-yellow color to the tofu in this delectable, cholesterol-free "egg" salad. You'll be amazed at how similar it is to "the real thing."

16 ounces firm tofu

1 cup Tofu 'Mayonnaise' (page 85)
½ cup celery (finely chopped)
2 tablespoons onion (finely chopped)
1 medium dill pickle (finely chopped)
2 teaspoons Dijon-style or stone-ground mustard
¾ teaspoon salt
¼ teaspoon ground turmeric
pinch of ground black pepper

1. Bring small pot of water to boil. Cut tofu in several pieces, and boil 5 minutes. Rinse tofu under cold water until cool.
2. Mash tofu in mixing bowl. Combine with remaining ingredients.
Note: Refrigerate leftovers and use within 7 days.
For serving ideas, see page 83.
Yield: 3-4 servings

Parsnip 'Crab' Salad

While most Americans have not yet come to appreciate parsnips, this sweet, nutty root vegetable takes center stage in this crunchy, yet delicate, "seafood" salad.

2 cups parsnips (peeled or scrubbed and grated)
3 tablespoons fresh lemon juice

1 cup celery (finely chopped)
1 cup Tofu 'Cutlets' (chopped) (page 94)
½ cup Tofu 'Mayonnaise' (page 85)
¼ cup roasted red pepper (chopped) (store-bought)
¼ cup onions (finely chopped)
¼ teaspoon salt
pinch of ground black pepper

1. Toss grated parsnips and lemon juice in bowl. Set aside 5-10 minutes. Add remaining ingredients and thoroughly combine.
Note: Refrigerate leftovers and use within 4 days.
For serving ideas, see page 83.
Yield: 3-4 servings

Garbanzo 'Tuna' Salad

A creamy, crunchy, and tangy tuna-free salad.
And, for a "fishy" flavor, stir in some Nori Flakes (page 92).

2 cups cooked garbanzo beans (coarsely mashed) (page 23)
¾ cup carrots (finely chopped)
½ cup each (finely chopped): celery and onions
2 medium dill pickles (finely chopped)
2 teaspoons Dijon-style or stone-ground mustard
1 teaspoon onion powder
1 medium garlic clove (finely chopped) or ½ teaspoon powder
¾ teaspoon salt

1 cup Tofu 'Mayonnaise' (page 85)

1. Combine all ingredients, except mayonnaise, in bowl. Add mayonnaise and combine thoroughly.
Note: Refrigerate leftovers and use within 7 days.
For serving ideas, see page 83.
Yield: 3-4 servings

'Sushi' Salad

This remarkably festive and "fishy" salad should please all who enjoy sushi.

4 cups cooked brown rice (page 25)

½ cup brown rice vinegar or apple cider vinegar
3 tablespoons sugar (i.e. evaporated cane juice)
¾ teaspoon salt

6 sheets toasted nori (torn in small pieces)
1 medium each (chopped): carrot and cucumber
1 medium red or yellow bell pepper (seeded and chopped)
1 recipe Tofu 'Cutlets' (chopped) (page 94) or ½ cup roasted pecans or
cashews (page 30)

1. Transfer rice to bowl and combine with vinegar, sugar, and salt.
2. Stir remaining ingredients into seasoned rice and combine.
Note: Refrigerate leftovers and use within 4 days.
Yield: 3-4 servings

Steamed Veggie Salad

Tender, steamed veggies are tossed with tangy dressing and studded with chewy, savory bits of baked tofu.

1 medium red onion (halved and sliced)
1 medium carrot (sliced diagonally)
2 cups cauliflower florets (cut in bite-sized pieces)

2 cups broccoli florets (cut in bite-sized pieces)
1 small zucchini (sliced diagonally)
1 medium red or yellow bell pepper (seeded and sliced)

1 recipe Tofu 'Cutlets' (sliced or chopped) (page 94)
Lemon Parsley Dressing (to taste) (page 63)

1. Place first 3 vegetables in steamer basket and steam several minutes. Add remaining vegetables and steam several minutes more, or until all the vegetables are as tender as desired.
2. Place steamed veggies in bowl and toss with tofu and dressing.
Note: Refrigerate leftovers and use within 4 days.
Yield: 3 servings

Collard 'Spaghetti'

Steamy, tender strands of cooked greens tossed with oil and salt. Heavenly!

1 bunch collard greens

olive oil or flax seed oil (to taste)
salt (to taste)

1. Rinse collards and remove stems with knife. Discard stems.
2. Stack leaves about 4 to 6 high. Roll up tightly into a long tube and slice into thin, spaghetti-like strands.
3. Unwrap and fluff the strands. Repeat with remaining collards.
4. Place thin strands in steamer basket and steam, covered, 5-7 minutes, or until strands are tender, but still a bit chewy.
5. In bowl, toss greens with oil and salt. Serve hot.
Note: Refrigerate leftovers and use within 4 days.
Yield: 2-3 servings

Coleslaw

Colorful and crunchy, this tangy cabbage salad actually gets even better with time. So, dress it, give it a few hours, then enjoy!

4 cups cabbage or bok choy (shredded)
1 cup green peas (fresh or frozen and thawed)
3 medium carrots (grated)
½ cup green onions (thinly sliced)
2 medium garlic cloves (finely chopped) or 1 teaspoon powder
1 teaspoon onion powder
½ teaspoon salt
pinch of ground black pepper

1 recipe Tofu 'Mayonnaise' (page 85)

1. Combine cabbage and all the remaining ingredients, except mayonnaise, in bowl. Add mayonnaise and combine thoroughly.
Note: Refrigerate leftovers and use within 5 days.
Yield: 4-6 servings

Rainbow Salad

A great "slaw." Nourishing, yet simple and vibrantly colorful!

2 cups green cabbage (shredded)
2 cups raw beets (peeled and grated)
2 cups carrots (grated)

Vinaigrette (to taste) (page 63)

1. Place vegetables in bowl and toss with dressing.
Note: Refrigerate leftovers and use within 5 days.
Yield: 3-4 servings
Variation: Add ½ cup chopped walnuts or ¼ cup sesame seeds to salad mix. For another color, top salad with small amount of grated daikon (large white radish).

Pasta Salad with Beans

This chilled, main-dish salad is pleasantly rich in color, flavor, texture, and especially nutrition.

2 cups uncooked whole-grain noodles (5-6 ounces)

1 tablespoon olive oil or flax seed oil
½ teaspoon salt

1 recipe Israeli Salad (see recipe below)

1. Cook noodles in boiling water in pot, until just tender, 8-10 minutes. Drain and return noodles to pot.
2. Toss noodles with oil and salt.
3. In bowl, combine noodles, salad, and dressing.
Note: Refrigerate leftovers and use within 5 days.
Yield: 4-5 servings

Israeli Salad

In tiny Israel, fresh produce is widely available. That's why vibrant salads are even eaten for breakfast. A great way to get the day started—anywhere!

1 cup cooked garbanzo beans (page 23)
2 medium tomatoes (chopped)
1 small cucumber (chopped)
½ cup green bell pepper (seeded and chopped)
¼ cup green onions (thinly sliced)

to taste: Lemon Parsley Dressing (page 63) or 'Honey' Mustard Dressing (page 65)

1. Combine all ingredients, except dressing, in bowl. Add dressing and combine.
Note: Refrigerate leftovers and use within 5 days.
Yield: 2-3 servings

Seeding a cucumber: A large cucumber may have big, unpalatable seeds. Seeding will make it more digestible and tasty. Peel the cucumber, if desired, then cut it in half lengthwise. Use a spoon to scrape out the seeds, then slice or chop the cucumber.

Kimchi Express

My quickie version of spicy Korean pickled cabbage—called Kimchi—will delight the senses with its traditional garlic, ginger, and hot pepper essences.

6 cups napa cabbage (coarsely chopped)
2 medium carrots (grated)
¾ cup green onions (thinly sliced)
¾ cup daikon radish (thinly sliced) (optional)
½ cup fresh cilantro (finely chopped) (optional)

½ cup brown rice vinegar or other vinegar
2 tablespoons fresh ginger (grated)
1 tablespoon maple syrup
1 tablespoon toasted sesame oil (optional)
1 teaspoon red pepper flakes (or to taste)
2-3 medium garlic cloves (finely chopped)
½ teaspoon salt

1. Combine vegetables in large bowl.
2. In small bowl, combine vinegar and remaining ingredients. Whisk and pour over vegetables. Toss well.

Note: Refrigerate leftovers and use within 5 days.

Yield: 6-8 servings

Variation: Replace napa cabbage with green or red cabbage or with bok choy.

Tabbouleh

My version of this popular Middle Eastern salad replaces highly-processed bulgur wheat with quinoa. Then I spruce it up with a perky dressing.

4 cups cooked quinoa (page 26)
2 medium tomatoes (chopped)
½ cup fresh parsley (finely chopped)
½ cup green onions (thinly sliced)
2 medium garlic cloves (finely chopped)
½ teaspoon salt
pinch of ground black pepper

Lemon Parsley Dressing (to taste) (page 63)

1. Combine all ingredients, except dressing, in large bowl. Add dressing and combine thoroughly.

Note: Refrigerate leftovers and use within 4 days.

Yield: 3-4 servings

1-2-3 Bean Salad

*The beans and veggies in this hearty, delectable salad make
a striking contrast of colors, flavors, and textures.*

**3 cups cooked beans (any combination of garbanzo, red kidney, and
black beans) (page 23)**
1 cup carrots (chopped)
¾ cup corn kernels (fresh or frozen and thawed)
½ cup green beans (cut in 1" pieces)
½ cup cherry tomatoes (cut in halves)
¼ cup green onions (thinly sliced)
1 tablespoon capers (rinsed) (optional)

Vinaigrette (to taste) (page 63)

1. Combine first 7 ingredients in bowl. Add dressing and toss well.
Note: To make crunchy vegetables more tender, briefly steam carrots, corn, and green beans in steamer basket for 1-2 minutes.
Beans should be cooked separately to avoid bleeding of colors between them.
Refrigerate leftovers and use within 5 days.
Yield: 4 servings

Taco Salad

*The familiar south-of-the-border "folded sandwich" is converted
into a hearty and tasty salad—loaded with protein, fiber, and flavor.*

1 medium bell pepper (seeded and sliced)
1 medium each: carrot (grated) and tomato (chopped)
1 medium avocado (peeled, pitted, and chopped) (optional)
½ cup red onions (finely chopped)

baked whole-grain tortilla chips (to taste)

4 cups romaine lettuce or other lettuce (chopped)
1 recipe 'Cheddar' Melt (page 73)
2 cups cooked black, pinto, or kidney beans (page 23)

Taco Dressing (to taste) (page 66)

1. Combine first 5 ingredients in bowl and set aside.
2. Distribute tortilla chips on plates and spread with lettuce, melted
cheddar, beans, and veggies. Serve with dollops of dressing.
Note: Refrigerate leftovers and use within 1 day.
Yield: 3-4 servings

Waldorf Salad

This wholesome re-make of a classic salad first served in New York City in 1896 is crisp and uncomplicated.

3 medium apples (cored and chopped)
2 medium carrots (finely chopped)
1 cup celery (finely chopped)
½ cup raisins or dried cranberries
½ cup walnuts (chopped)

1 cup Tofu 'Sour Cream' (page 86)
¼ cup maple syrup
1 teaspoon cinnamon
½ teaspoon salt

1. Combine first 5 ingredients in bowl.
2. In separate bowl combine sour cream with remaining 3 ingredients and toss with fruit and veggies.
Note: Refrigerate leftovers and use within 4 days.
Yield: 3-4 servings

Navy Maple Mustard Dressing

This creamy, tangy dressing is uniquely made with beans!

1 cup cooked navy or other white beans (page 23)
½ cup brown rice vinegar
¼ cup Dijon-style or stone-ground mustard
3 tablespoons maple syrup
1 tablespoon flax seed oil, olive oil, or canola oil
1 tablespoon flax seed meal (page 29)
1-2 medium garlic cloves
¼ teaspoon salt

1. Combine all ingredients in blender and blend until smooth.
Note: When chilled, dressing thickens considerably. Whisk in a little water to thin.
Refrigerate leftovers in glass jar and use within 7 days.
Yield: about 1¾ cups

Vinaigrette

Such a simple, quick dressing. Perfect over just about any type of salad.

¾ cup fresh lemon juice, apple cider vinegar, or other vinegar
3 tablespoons olive oil or flax seed oil
3 medium garlic cloves (finely chopped)
1 tablespoon sugar (i.e. evaporated cane juice)
½ teaspoon salt
pinch of ground black pepper

1. Combine all ingredients in jar and shake until well-mixed.
Note: Refrigerate leftovers in glass jar and use within 10 days.
Yield: about 1 cup
Variation: Add any or all of the following, to taste: nutritional yeast flakes, fresh chopped parsley or cilantro, dark miso, grated ginger, lemon zest, or Dijon-style or stone-ground mustard.

Lemon Parsley Dressing

An exceptionally perky dressing defined by its fusion of tart lemon and vibrant fresh parsley.

¾ cup water
½ cup fresh parsley (chopped)
¼ cup fresh lemon juice
2 tablespoons each: dark miso and brown rice vinegar
2 tablespoons olive oil or flax seed oil
½ teaspoon salt
pinch of ground black pepper

1. Combine all ingredients in blender and blend until smooth.
Note: Refrigerate leftovers in glass jar and use within 10 days.
Yield: about 1¼ cups
Variation: Replace parsley with fresh basil or cilantro.

Maple Tahini Dressing

A sweet and creamy, tangy dressing with rich tahini flavor.

½ cup each: tahini and brown rice vinegar
¼ cup water
2 tablespoons each: maple syrup and flax seed meal (page 29)
2 tablespoons flax seed oil or olive oil
½ teaspoon salt

1. Combine all ingredients in bowl and whisk until smooth.
Note: Refrigerate leftovers in glass jar and use within 10 days.
When chilled, dressing thickens considerably. Add a little water or vinegar and whisk to thin.
Yield: about 1½ cups
Variation: For **Orange Maple Tahini Dressing**, mix 2 tablespoons frozen orange juice concentrate with all ingredients.

Miso Tahini Dressing

What a great balance of flavors—sweet, sour, salty, cheesy,
and with a touch of sesame thrown in.

½ cup fresh lemon juice or brown rice vinegar
3 tablespoons dark or light miso
2 tablespoons olive oil or flax seed oil
2 tablespoons each: tahini and nutritional yeast flakes
2 medium garlic cloves
2 teaspoons maple syrup

1. Combine all ingredients in blender and blend until smooth.
Note: Refrigerate leftovers in glass jar and use within 10 days.
Yield: about 1 cup

Fresh lemon juice is bright, tart, and tangy. Bottled lemon juice may have an off-flavor, and is often stale or bitter. To make your own lemon juice, first scrub each lemon with soap and hot water to remove any bacteria that could be transferred to the fruit's flesh. Then slice each in half and use a hand-juicer ("citrus reamer") to extract the juice. Store juice in small glass jars in the refrigerator for up to 1 week, or in the freezer for up to 3 months. When freezing, allow 1" space on top for juice expansion.

'Honey' Mustard Dressing

Mustard lovers rejoice! Here is a zesty, sweet companion to everything.

½ cup maple syrup or agave nectar
¼ cup brown rice vinegar or apple cider vinegar
¼ cup Dijon-style or stone-ground mustard
2 tablespoons olive oil or flax seed oil
2 medium garlic cloves
½ teaspoon salt
pinch of ground black pepper

1. Combine all ingredients in blender and blend until smooth.
Note: Refrigerate leftovers in glass jar and use within 10 days.
Yield: about 1¼ cups

Ranch Dressing

A tangy, creamy dressing that gets quite a flavor boost from the dill.

1 recipe Tofu 'Sour Cream' (page 86)
3 tablespoons brown rice vinegar or apple cider vinegar
2 teaspoons Dijon-style or stone-ground mustard
2 medium garlic cloves
1 teaspoon dried dill or 1 tablespoon fresh dill
½ teaspoon salt

1. Combine all ingredients in blender and blend until smooth.
Note: Refrigerate leftovers in glass jar and use within 7 days.
Yield: about 1½ cups

Green Goddess Dressing

A dressing with a delicate green hue and spirited herb flavor.

1 cup Tofu 'Mayonnaise' (page 85)
½ cup fresh parsley (chopped)
¼ cup green onions (sliced)
2 tablespoons fresh lemon juice or brown rice vinegar
2 tablespoons water
1-2 medium garlic cloves

1. Combine all ingredients in blender and blend until smooth.
Note: Refrigerate leftovers in glass jar and use within 7 days.
Yield: about 1¼ cups

Thousand Island Dressing

Creamy pink, faintly sweet, and studded with crunchy bits of pickle.

1 cup Tofu 'Mayonnaise' (page 85)
¼ cup Ketchup (page 87 or store-bought)
¼ cup dill pickle (finely chopped)
1-2 medium garlic cloves (finely chopped)

1. Combine all ingredients in bowl. Stir until smooth.
Note: Refrigerate leftovers in glass jar and use within 7 days.
Yield: about 1½ cups

Taco Dressing

Add a Southwestern flair to any salad or savory dish with this peppy dressing.

1 cup Tofu 'Mayonnaise' (page 85)
2 medium tomatoes (finely chopped)
¼ cup fresh lime or lemon juice or apple cider vinegar
2 teaspoons chili powder (or more, to taste)
½ teaspoon salt
¼ teaspoon ground cayenne pepper (or more, to taste)

1. Combine all ingredients in bowl. Stir until smooth.
Note: Refrigerate leftovers in glass jar and use within 5 days.
Yield: about 1½ cups

French Dressing

A dazzling, classic dressing that's sweet and tart, yet savory, too.

2 medium tomatoes (chopped)
¼ cup brown rice vinegar or apple cider vinegar
2 tablespoons olive oil or flax seed oil
2 tablespoons flax seed meal (page 29)
2 tablespoons fresh lemon or lime juice
1 tablespoon maple syrup or agave nectar
2 medium garlic cloves
½ teaspoon salt

1. Combine all ingredients in blender and blend until smooth.
Note: Refrigerate leftovers in glass jar and use within 5 days.
Yield: about 1½ cups

5 'Cheesy'

'Mozzarella Bean Cheese'

Low-fat and high-fiber, this delicately tart cheese is mostly beans and water!
Yet, it's firm enough to grate, cube, and slice. Like "the real thing."

1½ cups cold water
5 tablespoons agar flakes (or for agar powder see glossary)

1 cup cooked navy or other white beans (page 23)
3 tablespoons fresh lemon juice
2 tablespoons cashew butter
1 tablespoon each: onion powder and canola oil
¾ teaspoon salt

1. Combine agar and water in pot. Bring to boil over medium-high heat, stirring bottom of pot often to prevent sticking. Reduce heat and simmer until agar dissolves, about 5 minutes, stirring often.

2. Place remaining ingredients in blender. Start blender and slowly pour hot agar mixture through center lid opening of blender. Blend until smooth.

3. Pour liquid cheese mixture into glass container and chill uncovered at least 30 minutes in refrigerator. Then, cover and chill several hours to allow cheese to firm up.

Note: Refrigerate leftovers and use within 7 days.

For serving ideas, see page 69.

Yield: about 16 ounces

Variation: For **'Mozzarella Nut Cheese'**, replace beans with ½ cup cashew butter.

The **hard cheeses** in this book are made without saturated animal fat or dairy protein (casein). This is why they're softer than hard dairy cheeses and don't stretch or melt like "the real things." However, when grated and tossed with a little oil and combined with hot food, these vegan cheeses do soften and get melty—as when they're tossed with hot grains, pastas, or veggies. And, these dairy-free cheeses will brown (rather quickly!) when put under the broiler.

Feel free to experiment with the gelling agent agar (flakes or powder) using either more or less to make the cheeses harder or softer. And, let your imagination go as you toss your favorite herbs and seasonings into the blender to create exotic new cheese flavors.

'Provolone Bean Cheese'

This smoky bean "cheese" is free of cholesterol and saturated animal fat.
It's remarkably good, especially cubed, sliced, and grated.

1½ cups cold water
5 tablespoons agar flakes (or for agar powder see glossary)

1 cup cooked navy or other white beans (page 23)
2 tablespoons each: fresh lemon juice and tahini
1 tablespoon toasted sesame oil
2-3 medium garlic cloves or 1½ teaspoons powder
¾ teaspoon salt
½ teaspoon liquid smoke
pinch of ground black pepper

1. Combine agar and water in pot. Bring to boil over medium-high heat, stirring bottom of pot often to prevent sticking. Reduce heat and simmer until agar dissolves, about 5 minutes, stirring often.

2. Place remaining ingredients in blender. Start blender and slowly pour hot agar mixture through center lid opening of blender. Blend until smooth.

3. Pour liquid cheese mixture into glass container and chill uncovered at least 30 minutes in refrigerator. Then, cover and chill several hours to allow cheese to firm up.

Note: Refrigerate leftovers and use within 7 days.

For serving ideas, see below.

Yield: about 16 ounces

Variation: For **'Provolone Nut Cheese'**, replace beans with ½ cup cashew butter.

Some ways to enjoy these hard cheeses

- sliced and layered over crackers or bread
- grated and spread over pizza
- cubed and tossed with green salad
- grated and tossed with hot or cold grains, noodles, or veggies
- sliced and layered over burgers and casseroles (then briefly broiled to melt and brown)
- cubed and served on toothpicks with apple or pear wedges

'Cheddar Bean Cheese'

A tangy, solid cheese with familiar orange color. Like other firm cheeses, it's great cubed, grated, or tossed with salads, grains, pastas, and hot vegetables.

1½ cups cold water
5 tablespoons agar flakes (or for agar powder see glossary)

1 cup cooked navy or other white beans (page 23)
¾ cup roasted red pepper (chopped) (store-bought)
3 tablespoons fresh lemon juice
3 tablespoons nutritional yeast flakes
2 tablespoons tahini or cashew butter
1 tablespoon Dijon-style or stone-ground mustard
1 tablespoon toasted sesame oil
1½ teaspoons onion powder
2 medium garlic cloves or 1 teaspoon garlic powder
¾ teaspoon salt

1. Combine agar and water in pot. Bring to boil over medium-high heat, stirring bottom of pot often to prevent sticking. Reduce heat and simmer until agar dissolves, about 5 minutes, stirring often.

2. Place remaining ingredients in blender. Start blender and slowly pour hot agar mixture through center lid opening of blender. Blend until smooth.

3. Pour liquid cheese mixture into glass container and chill uncovered at least 30 minutes in refrigerator. Then, cover and chill several hours to allow cheese to firm up.

Note: Refrigerate leftovers and use within 7 days.

For serving ideas, see page 69.

Yield: about 16 ounces

Homemade cooked beans are easily frozen and can be used weeks later to create a quick meal. Let cooked beans cool, then drain, and transfer to a 2 cup glass jar (or plastic container). Leave about 1" space at the top for bean expansion. To "quickly" defrost frozen beans stored in glass, immerse the jar in a pot of **cold** water. Then place the pot on the stove, on low heat, and simmer until beans have thawed. An alternate method is to leave the jar or plastic container on the countertop for several hours, or until thawed.

'Salami Cheese'

Talk about boldly-seasoned cheeses. This "meaty" one, with its red hue and passionate garlic essence, is mouth-watering on crackers or tossed in salads.

1½ cups cold water
5 tablespoons agar flakes (or for agar powder see glossary)

1 cup cooked red kidney beans (page 23)
3 tablespoons fresh lemon juice
2 tablespoons tahini or cashew butter
1 tablespoon toasted sesame oil
1 tablespoon onion powder
4-6 medium garlic cloves
¾ teaspoon salt
½ teaspoon liquid smoke
pinch of ground black pepper

1. Combine agar and water in pot. Bring to boil over medium-high heat, stirring bottom of pot often to prevent sticking. Reduce heat and simmer until agar dissolves, about 5 minutes, stirring often.

2. Place remaining ingredients in blender. Start blender and slowly pour hot agar mixture through center lid opening of blender. Blend until smooth.

3. Pour liquid cheese mixture into glass container and chill uncovered at least 30 minutes in refrigerator. Then, cover and chill several hours to allow cheese to firm up.

Note: Refrigerate leftovers and use within 7 days.

For serving ideas, see page 69.

Yield: about 16 ounces

'Cheesy' Brown Rice

Brown rice and "cheese" mingle compatibly in this tasty dish.

3 cups cooked brown rice or other whole grains (page 25)
1 tablespoon flax seed oil or olive oil
½ teaspoon salt

½ recipe 'Mozzarella Bean Cheese' (grated) (page 68)

1. In bowl, combine first 3 ingredients. Add cheese and toss.

Note: Refrigerate leftovers and use within 7 days.

Yield: 3-4 servings

Variation: Replace bean cheese with other hard "cheese."

'Mozzarella' Melt

A creamy melt, heavenly over noodles, grains, and hot veggies.

2 cups non-dairy milk
1 cup cooked navy or other white beans (page 23)
3 tablespoons each: cashew butter, fresh lemon juice, and arrowroot
1 tablespoon canola oil
1 tablespoon onion powder
¾ teaspoon salt

1. Place all ingredients in blender and blend until smooth.

2. Transfer blended mixture to a pot and bring to slow simmer over medium heat stirring occasionally. Continue simmering until thick and smooth, about 5 minutes, stirring constantly.

Note: Refrigerate leftovers and use within 7 days.

Leftovers will firm up to a cream cheese texture. To return to melt texture, heat leftovers in a pot over low heat, stirring frequently.

Yield: about 2½ cups

'Provolone' Melt

Thick, creamy, and smoky. Enjoy this "cheese" melt over grains, baked or steamed potatoes, or spread on burgers or casseroles.

2 cups non-dairy milk
1 cup cooked navy or other white beans (page 23)
3 tablespoons each: tahini, fresh lemon juice, and arrowroot
1 tablespoon toasted sesame oil
2 medium garlic cloves or 1 teaspoon powder
1 teaspoon onion powder
¾ teaspoon salt
½ teaspoon liquid smoke
pinch of ground black pepper

1. Place all ingredients in blender and blend until smooth.

2. Transfer blended mixture to a pot and bring to slow simmer over medium heat stirring occasionally. Continue simmering until thick and smooth, about 5 minutes, stirring constantly.

Note: Refrigerate leftovers and use within 7 days.

Leftovers will firm up to a cream cheese texture. To return to melt texture, heat leftovers in a pot over low heat, stirring frequently.

Yield: about 2½ cups

'Cheddar' Melt

A thick, orange "cheese" sauce that bursts with flavor—not fat. It pleads for tortilla chips ('Nachos', see below) or noodles (Mac & 'Cheese', page 74).

2 cups non-dairy milk
1 cup roasted red pepper (chopped) (store-bought)
¼ cup tahini or cashew butter
3 tablespoons each: fresh lemon juice and arrowroot
3 tablespoons nutritional yeast flakes
1 tablespoon toasted sesame oil
1 tablespoon Dijon-style or stone-ground mustard
2 medium garlic cloves or 1 teaspoon powder
1½ teaspoons onion powder
¾ teaspoon salt

1. Place all ingredients in blender and blend until smooth.

2. Transfer blended mixture to a pot and bring to slow simmer over medium heat stirring occasionally. Continue simmering until thick and smooth, about 5 minutes, stirring constantly.

Note: Refrigerate leftovers and use within 7 days.

Leftovers will firm up to a cream cheese texture. To return to melt texture, heat leftovers in a pot over low heat, stirring frequently.

Yield: about 2½ cups

'Nachos'

Crunchy finger-food dripping with the most wholesome "cheddar" sauce ever. Add a big green salad, and you've got dinner!

1 bag (7 ounces) baked whole-grain tortilla chips

1 recipe 'Cheddar' Melt (see above)
2 cups cooked black beans (page 23)
¼ cup green onions (thinly sliced)
2 medium tomatoes (chopped)

1 recipe Tofu 'Sour Cream' (optional) (page 86)

1. Spread tortilla chips on large serving platter or plate.

2. Cover chips with half of melted cheese, followed by beans, green onions, and tomatoes. Top with remaining cheese.

3. Serve now, or place under broiler for quick sizzle, before topping with sour cream, if being used.

Yield: 3-4 servings

Mac & 'Cheese'

Whichever sauce you use will transform the noodles into an incredibly satisfying and healthful culinary experience.

3 cups uncooked whole-grain noodles (about 8 ounces)

1 tablespoon olive oil or canola oil
½ teaspoon salt

1 recipe 'Cheddar' Melt (page 73), 'Provolone' Melt (page 72), or 'Mozzarella' Melt (page 72)

1. Cook noodles in boiling water 8-10 minutes, or until tender. Drain and return to pot.
2. Toss noodles with oil and salt.
3. Add cheese melt to noodles and mix. If desired cook briefly over low heat until noodles and cheese are thoroughly warmed.
Note: Refrigerate leftovers and use within 7 days.
Yield: 4-5 servings

Tofu 'Cottage Cheese'

A mild-flavored curd "cheese" with a delightfully moist texture. It welcomes the addition of chopped fruit or veggies.

16 ounces firm tofu

1 cup Tofu 'Sour Cream' (page 86)
½ teaspoon salt

1. Bring small pot of water to boil. Cut tofu in several pieces, and boil 5 minutes. Rinse tofu under cold water until cool.
2. Place tofu in mixing bowl and mash with fork. Add Tofu 'Sour Cream' and salt and thoroughly combine.
Note: Refrigerate leftovers and use within 7 days.
Yield: 3-4 servings

Broccoli 'Quiche'

This "quiche" is creamy and rich without the usual eggs and cream. And, it's crustless. So, you get to eat more of the really good stuff—broccoli and beans.

4 cups raw broccoli florets (chopped)
1 medium onion (chopped)
2 cups cooked navy or other white beans (mashed) (page 23)
1½ cups mushrooms (chopped)
½ cup roasted red pepper (chopped) (store-bought)

1 cup non-dairy milk
¼ cup garbanzo bean flour or brown rice flour
3 tablespoons each: arrowroot, lemon juice, and tahini
1 tablespoon toasted sesame oil
2 teaspoons Dijon-style or stone-ground mustard
1½ teaspoons each: garlic powder and onion powder
1 teaspoon each: dried thyme, liquid smoke, and salt
¼ teaspoon each: ground black pepper and ground turmeric

1. Preheat oven to 350°.
2. In bowl, combine first 5 ingredients.
3. Place remaining ingredients in blender and blend until smooth.
4. Pour blended ingredients into bowl of broccoli mixture. Mix well and transfer to oiled 9" pie plate (or similar-sized baking dish).
5. Bake 60 minutes. Let quiche stand 10-15 minutes before serving.
Note: Refrigerate leftovers and use within 4 days or freeze.
Yield: 4-5 servings

Sesame 'Parmesan'

Add a richness and depth of flavor to any dish sprinkled with this pale-golden, granular "Parmesan." Or, just let it melt in your mouth.

½ recipe Roasted Seeds (sesame seeds) (page 30)
¼ cup nutritional yeast flakes
1 teaspoon each: garlic powder and onion powder
¼ teaspoon salt

1. Place all ingredients in blender and blend until coarsely ground, stopping to stir mixture, as necessary.
Note: Refrigerate leftovers and use within 2 weeks.
Yield: about 1 cup

Tofu 'Cream Cheese'

This is pretty close to "the real thing"—but without any cholesterol or saturated animal fat. It's smooth, creamy, and mildly tangy.

8 ounces firm tofu

¼ cup fresh lemon juice
1 tablespoon canola oil
½ teaspoon salt

1½ cups cold water
2 tablespoons agar flakes (or for agar powder see glossary)

2 tablespoons arrowroot mixed with 2 tablespoons cold water

1. Bring pot of water to boil. Cut tofu in several pieces, and boil 5 minutes. Rinse tofu under cold water until cool.

2. Place tofu in blender with next 3 ingredients. Set aside.

3. Combine agar and water in pot. Bring to boil over medium-high heat, stirring bottom of pot often to prevent sticking. Reduce heat and simmer until agar dissolves, about 5 minutes, stirring often.

4. Stir arrowroot mixture into simmering agar mixture. Continue stirring until mixture thickens, about 10-15 seconds.

5. Start blender and slowly pour hot, agar-arrowroot mixture through center lid opening of blender. Blend until smooth.

6. Pour mixture into glass container. Chill several hours to firm up.

7. Whisk cheese for whipped texture, or leave as is for firm texture.

Note: Refrigerate leftovers and use within 7 days.

Yield: about 2 cups

Variation: Add a small amount of fresh or dried herbs (i.e. parsley, chives, basil, or dill) to step 2.

6 Dips, Sauces, & Condiments

Hummus

This tangy, low-fat version of the classic, oil-rich Middle Eastern chickpea dip gets its richness from the tahini.

2 cups cooked garbanzo beans (page 23)
¼ cup water
¼ cup apple cider vinegar or fresh lemon juice
2 tablespoons each: tahini and soy sauce
1 medium garlic clove or ½ teaspoon garlic powder
½ teaspoon ground cayenne pepper (optional)

¼ cup green onions (thinly sliced)

1. Place all ingredients, except green onions, in blender and blend until smooth, adding a little more water to thin, if desired.
2. Transfer mixture to bowl and stir in green onions.
Note: Refrigerate leftovers in glass container and use within 4 days. For serving ideas, see page 83.
Yield: about 2 cups
Variation: For **Roasted Red Pepper Hummus** add ½ cup chopped roasted red pepper (store-bought) and ½ teaspoon ground cumin to step 1.

Pesto

This wholesome, low-fat pesto is a healthy departure from the other creamy Italian sauces loaded with oil and Parmesan.

2 cups fresh basil or arugula
½ cup walnuts or other raw nuts
½ cup fresh parsley or cilantro (finely chopped)
¼ cup nutritional yeast flakes
¼ cup each: fresh lemon juice and water
¼ cup cashew or almond butter
2 medium garlic cloves (finely chopped) or 1 teaspoon powder
2 tablespoons olive oil, canola oil, or other plain oil
½ teaspoon salt
pinch of ground black pepper

1. Place all ingredients in blender and blend until smooth, adding a little more water, as necessary, for smooth consistency.
Note: Refrigerate leftovers in glass container and use within 2 days.
Yield: about 1½ cups

Baba Ghanoush

*Popular throughout the Middle East, this roasted eggplant dip
is positively delectable—and addictive.*

2 medium eggplants (any variety, about 1½ pounds total)

¼ cup fresh parsley or cilantro (finely chopped)
2 tablespoons each: tahini and fresh lemon juice
1 tablespoon olive oil or canola oil
1 medium garlic clove (finely chopped) or ½ teaspoon powder
½ teaspoon each: ground cumin and salt
pinch of ground black pepper

1. Preheat oven to 375°.
2. Cut eggplants in half lengthwise and place cut-side down on oiled baking sheet.
3. Bake 1 hour or until eggplants are completely soft and collapsed.
4. When eggplants have cooked, scrape pulp out of skin into bowl. Stir in remaining ingredients until smooth.
Note: Refrigerate leftovers in glass container and use within 2 days. For serving ideas, see page 83.
Yield: about 1½ cups

Southwestern Black Bean Dip

*Black beans are a great fit for this tantalizing dip.
Pinto beans or red kidney beans would work nicely, too.*

2 cups cooked black beans (page 23)
¾ cup Veggie Salsa (page 80 or store-bought)
1 tablespoon fresh lemon juice or apple cider vinegar
½ teaspoon each: ground cumin and salt
pinch of ground black pepper

½ cup onions (finely chopped)
1 medium garlic clove (finely chopped) or ½ teaspoon powder

1. Place all ingredients, except onions and garlic, in blender and blend until smooth.
2. Transfer blender mixture to bowl and stir in onions and garlic.
Note: Refrigerate leftovers in glass container and use within 4 days. For serving ideas, see page 83.
Yield: about 2 cups

Veggie Salsa

*This salsa's got it all. Think of it as a juicy chopped salad
or as a mildly spicy sauce or even as a relish or a dip.*

2 medium tomatoes (chopped)
¾ cup bell pepper (halved, seeded, and chopped)
¼ cup green onions (thinly sliced)
2 tablespoons fresh parsley, basil or cilantro (finely chopped)
2 tablespoons fresh lemon or lime juice
1 medium garlic clove (finely chopped) or ½ teaspoon powder
¼ teaspoon each: chili powder, ground cumin, and salt
pinch of ground black pepper

1. Thoroughly combine all ingredients in bowl.
Note: Refrigerate leftovers in glass container and use within 4 days.
Yield: about 2 cups
Variation: For **Black Bean & Corn Salsa**, combine 2 cups cooked
black beans (page 23) and 1 cup fresh or frozen corn kernels (thawed)
with all ingredients.

Mango Salsa

*A remarkable tropical salsa that easily outshines any commercially-prepared
rival. For added heat, stir in a little finely chopped jalapeño pepper.*

2 cups ripe mangoes (peeled and chopped)
¾ cup cucumber (peeled and seeded, if desired, and chopped)
½ cup red onions (chopped)
½ cup red bell pepper (halved, seeded, and chopped)
¼ cup fresh lemon or lime juice
¼ cup fresh parsley, basil, or cilantro (finely chopped)
1 tablespoon olive oil or flax seed oil
¼ teaspoon salt
pinch of ground black pepper

1. Thoroughly combine all ingredients in bowl.
Note: Refrigerate leftovers in glass container and use within 4 days.
Yield: about 3 cups
Variation: Replace mangoes with ripe peaches or nectarines.

Broccoli 'Guacamole'

Broccoli replaces avocado to make this light and tasty dip not only low in fat, but packed with calcium.

1 small potato (cut in chunks)

3 cups broccoli florets (cut in bite-sized pieces)

¼ cup each: fresh lemon juice and water
1 tablespoon olive oil or canola oil
2 medium garlic cloves (finely chopped) or 1 teaspoon powder
1 teaspoon chili powder
½ teaspoon each: salt and ground cumin
pinch of ground black pepper

2 medium tomatoes (finely chopped)
3 tablespoons onions (finely chopped)

1. Place potato chunks in steamer basket and steam until tender when pierced with fork, about 10 minutes.

2. Transfer steamed potatoes to blender. Set aside.

3. Place broccoli in steamer basket and steam 3 minutes.

4. In blender, blend potatoes, broccoli, and remaining ingredients, except tomatoes and onion, until smooth.

5. Transfer mixture to bowl. Add chopped tomatoes and onion and thoroughly combine.

Note: Refrigerate leftovers in glass container and use within 1 day.

For serving ideas, see page 83.

Yield: about 2 cups

'Cheesy' Lentil Dip

Spicy, earthy lentils are blended with tender, cooked onions to create a delightfully creamy texture embracing sweet, cheesy, and garlic overtones.

1 medium onion (chopped)
¼ cup water

2 cups cooked brown lentils (page 24)
¼ cup nutritional yeast flakes
2 tablespoons soy sauce
1 tablespoon toasted sesame oil
2 medium garlic cloves (finely chopped) or 1 teaspoon powder
pinch of ground black pepper

1. Place onions and water in pot. Bring to boil over medium heat, reduce heat, cover, and simmer 10 minutes, or until onions are tender. Stir occasionally.

2. Transfer onions and cooking water to blender and blend with remaining ingredients.

Note: Refrigerate leftovers in glass container and use within 4 days. For serving ideas, see page 83.

Yield: about 3 cups

Walnut & Lentil Pâté

Lentils and walnuts mingle flavors and textures in this delicious, satiny-smooth spread.

1½ cups cooked brown lentils (page 24)
1 cup raw walnuts
¼ cup water
2 tablespoons each: soy sauce and fresh lemon juice
2 medium garlic cloves
1 tablespoon olive oil or flax seed oil
pinch of ground black pepper

1. Place all ingredients in blender and blend until smooth, adding more water, as necessary, for smooth consistency.

Note: Refrigerate leftovers in glass container and use within 4 days. For serving ideas, see page 83.

Yield: about 2 cups

Variation: Replace cooked lentils with equal amount of cooked navy, pinto, or other beans.

Greek Yellow Split Pea Dip

*The yellow split peas impart a unique natural sweetness and creaminess
to this popular Greek appetizer.*

1 cup dried yellow split peas

2½ cups water
½ cup onions (chopped)
2 medium garlic cloves (finely chopped) or 1 teaspoon powder
1 teaspoon salt

¼ cup red onions (finely chopped)
3 tablespoons fresh parsley (finely chopped)
2 tablespoons fresh lemon or lime juice
1 tablespoon olive oil or canola oil
pinch of ground black pepper

1. Pick through peas, discarding any foreign matter. Rinse peas.

2. Combine peas with next 4 ingredients in pot. Bring to boil over
medium-high heat, reduce heat, cover, and simmer 45 minutes.

3. Uncover pot, simmer additional 10-15 minutes, stirring often,
until mixture thickens.

4. Transfer mixture to bowl and stir in remaining 5 ingredients.
Note: Allow dip to cool a little before serving.
Refrigerate leftovers in glass container and use within 4 days.
Yield: about 3 cups

Dips... ways to celebrate

- Serve with tortillas, pita wedges, chips, or crackers.
- Toss with hot or cold pasta or grains.
- Use as a filling for burritos and vegetarian sushi.
- Fill lettuce or collard leaves (raw or steamed), then roll.
- Spread on a baked pizza crust with all the toppings.
- Pile on a bagel or bread with onion or tomato slices.
- Fill grooves of celery or hollowed-out cucumbers.
- Serve as a salad dressing, thinned with vinegar.
- Dollop on baked potatoes or baked yams.
- Serve on a vegetable platter with slices or sticks of:
carrot, celery, bell pepper, jicama, turnip, cucumber, and
zucchini. And be sure to include cherry tomatoes, raw or
steamed broccoli or cauliflower florets, and sugar snap peas.

Tempeh & Mushroom Pâté

While "true pâtés" call for goose livers, this version relies upon tempeh and mushrooms for its lush texture and complex, meaty flavor.

8 ounces tempeh (cut in chunks)
1 cup mushrooms (sliced)

2 tablespoons each: water and tahini
1 tablespoon each: soy sauce, apple cider vinegar, dark miso, and toasted sesame oil
½ teaspoon liquid smoke (optional)
pinch of ground black pepper

3 tablespoons onions (finely chopped)
1 medium garlic clove (finely chopped) or ½ teaspoon powder

1. Steam tempeh and mushrooms in steamer basket 15 minutes.
2. Remove tempeh, and mash in bowl. Finely chop steamed mushrooms and combine with mashed tempeh.
3. In separate bowl, combine remaining ingredients, except onions and garlic, and stir into tempeh-mushroom mixture. Stir in onions and garlic and mash until mixture is smooth.

Note: Refrigerate leftovers in glass container and use within 2 days.
For serving ideas, see page 83.
Yield: about 2 cups

French Onion Dip

This zesty version of the classic dip is whipped up with tofu and natural seasonings, not with cholesterol and artificial flavors.

1 recipe Tofu 'Sour Cream' (page 86)
¼ cup red onions (finely chopped)
1 tablespoon onion powder
1 medium garlic clove (finely chopped) or ½ teaspoon powder
pinch of ground black pepper

1. Thoroughly combine all ingredients in bowl.

Note: Refrigerate leftovers in glass container and use within 4 days.
For serving ideas, see page 83.
Yield: about ½ cup

Tofu 'Mayonnaise'

The healthiest, lowest-fat natural mayo on earth!
Use this tangy tofu mayo to replace "the real thing" everywhere.

8 ounces firm tofu

¼ cup each: apple cider vinegar and water
1 tablespoon canola oil or olive oil
1½ teaspoons Dijon-style or stone-ground mustard
½ teaspoon salt

1. Bring pot of water to boil. Cut tofu in several pieces, and boil 5 minutes. Rinse tofu under cold water until cool.
2. Place tofu and remaining ingredients in blender and blend until smooth, adding more water as necessary for smooth consistency.
Note: Refrigerate leftovers in glass jar and use within 7 days.
Tofu 'Mayonnaise' will thicken when chilled.
Yield: about 1½ cups
Variation: For **Tofu 'Aioli'**, add 2-3 medium garlic cloves to blender and blend with all ingredients until smooth.

Tofu 'Tartar Sauce'

A mayo-based sauce punctuated with tasty morsels of pickles.
Use it on any dish that calls for a tangy, creamy sauce.

1 cup Tofu 'Mayonnaise' (see recipe above)
1½ medium dill pickles (finely chopped)
2 tablespoons fresh lemon juice
1 tablespoon capers (rinsed) (optional)
2 teaspoons Dijon-style or stone-ground mustard
1 medium garlic clove (finely chopped)

1. Combine all ingredients in bowl and mix thoroughly.
Note: Refrigerate leftovers in glass jar and use within 7 days.
Yield: about 1¼ cups

Tofu 'Sour Cream'

With the tartness and body of sour cream, this great-tasting tofu version eliminates all cholesterol and saturated fat.

8 ounces firm tofu

¼ cup each: fresh lemon juice and water
1 tablespoon canola oil or olive oil
½ teaspoon salt

1. Bring pot of water to boil. Cut tofu in several pieces, and boil 5 minutes. Rinse tofu under cold water until cool.
2. Place tofu and remaining ingredients in blender and blend until smooth, adding more water as necessary for smooth consistency.
Note: Refrigerate leftovers in glass jar and use within 7 days.
Tofu 'Sour Cream' will thicken when chilled.
Yield: about 1½ cups
Variation: For more tart flavor, add 2 tablespoons fresh lemon juice to step 2.

Navy 'Sour Cream'

This sour cream is full of beans! It's great on cooked grains and pasta.

2 cups cooked navy or other white beans (page 23)

¼ cup each: fresh lemon juice and water
2 tablespoons cashew butter
1 tablespoon canola oil or olive oil
½ teaspoon salt

1. Place all ingredients in blender and blend until smooth, adding more water, as necessary, for desired consistency.
Note: If using hot, just-cooked beans, increase beans by ½ cup.
When chilled, 'Sour Cream' thickens considerably. Whisk in a little water to thin.
Refrigerate leftovers in glass jar and use within 7 days.
Yield: about 2 cups
Variation: Replace navy beans with cooked red lentils, soybeans, or garbanzo beans. For more tart flavor, add 2 tablespoons fresh lemon juice to step 1.

Ketchup

A thick, homemade spicy sauce that outshines the sugary commercial brands.

½ cup tomato paste
¼ cup water
1½ tablespoons brown rice vinegar or apple cider vinegar
1½ tablespoons maple syrup or agave nectar
½ teaspoon each: garlic powder, onion powder, and salt

1. Combine all ingredients in bowl and whisk until smooth.
Note: Refrigerate leftovers in glass jar and use within 7 days.
Yield: about 1 cup

Bar-B-Q Sauce

Tangy, sweet, and smoky.

½ cup tomato paste
¼ cup apple cider vinegar or other vinegar
1 tablespoon each: soy sauce, toasted sesame oil, molasses, and Dijon-
    style or stone-ground mustard
1 teaspoon chili powder
½ teaspoon each: garlic powder, onion powder, salt, liquid smoke,
    and sugar (i.e. evaporated cane juice)

1. Combine all ingredients in bowl and mix thoroughly.
Note: Refrigerate leftovers in glass jar and use within 7 days.
Yield: about 1 cup

Pizza Sauce

A simple, flavorful way to grace a wholesome pizza (page 106).

½ cup tomato paste
¼ cup water
½ teaspoon each: dried basil, garlic powder, onion powder, dried
    oregano, salt, and sugar (i.e. evaporated cane juice)

1. Combine all ingredients in bowl and mix thoroughly.
Note: Refrigerate leftovers in glass jar and use within 7 days.
Yield: about ¾ cup

Black Bean Sauce

A fusion of black beans and distinctive seasonings. The result is a rich, savory sauce to complement any grain or veggie dish.

2 cups cooked black beans (page 23)
½ cup water
¼ cup cashew butter, almond butter, or tahini
2 tablespoons each: soy sauce and fresh lemon juice
1 medium garlic clove (chopped)
1 teaspoon onion powder
½ teaspoon each: ground cumin and salt

1. Place all ingredients in blender and blend until smooth, adding more water as necessary for smooth consistency.

2. Transfer mixture to pot and bring to simmer over medium heat, stirring frequently. Add water to thin, if desired.

Note: Refrigerate leftovers in glass container and use within 5 days.

Yield: about 2 cups

Teriyaki Sauce

A dazzling sauce, alive with fresh ginger and garlic, that will perk up any stir-fry, grain, or veggie dish.

½ cup water
3 tablespoons frozen orange juice concentrate (thawed)
3 tablespoons fresh lemon or lime juice or brown rice vinegar
3 tablespoons soy sauce
3 tablespoons maple syrup or agave nectar
1½ tablespoons arrowroot mixed in 1½ tablespoons cold water
1 tablespoon each: toasted sesame oil and fresh ginger (grated)
2 medium garlic cloves (finely chopped)

1. In pot, combine all ingredients and bring to simmer over medium heat, stirring frequently until thick. To thicken sauce further, stir in a little more arrowroot-water mixture.

Note: Refrigerate leftovers in glass jar. Use within 7 days or freeze.

Yield: about 1½ cups

Tempeh Spaghetti Sauce

*Thick and chunky, this "meaty" sauce is packed with protein and fiber.
Toss with cooked whole-grain pasta for one hearty meal!*

8 ounces tempeh (cut in ½" cubes or grated)
3 cups pasta sauce
¾ cup water
1 medium onion (chopped)
1 medium carrot (finely chopped)
1 tablespoon toasted sesame oil or olive oil
2 teaspoons dried basil
1 teaspoon each: garlic powder and onion powder
½ teaspoon salt

1. Combine all ingredients in pot. Bring to simmer over medium heat, stirring occasionally. Reduce heat, cover, and simmer 30 minutes, stirring occasionally.

Note: Refrigerate leftovers in glass jar. Use within 4 days or freeze.

Yield: 4-5 servings

Variation: For **Tofu Spaghetti Sauce**, replace tempeh with 12 ounces firm tofu (cut in ½" cubes or crumbled).

Peanut Sauce

*Delectably racy, this sauce is great over pasta, grains, and veggie dishes.
Or, chill and use to dress salad greens.*

1¼ cups water
½ cup peanut butter
3 tablespoons brown rice vinegar or apple cider vinegar
2 tablespoons soy sauce
1½ tablespoons sugar (i.e. evaporated cane juice)
1½ tablespoons toasted sesame oil
1-2 medium garlic cloves (chopped) or 1½ teaspoons powder
1½ teaspoons ground ginger
½ teaspoon ground cayenne pepper

1. Place all ingredients in blender and blend until smooth. Transfer mixture to pot. Bring to simmer over medium heat, stirring frequently, until thick and bubbling. Add water to thin, if desired.

Note: Refrigerate leftovers in glass jar. Use within 7 days.

Yield: about 2 cups

Thai Sauce

Toss with hot noodles and veggies—and you've got 'Pad Thai' (page 52).

¾ cup dried shiitake mushrooms (crumbled, about ½ ounce)

1¼ cups water
2 tablespoons fresh parsley or cilantro (finely chopped)
1 tablespoon fresh ginger (grated)
2 medium garlic cloves (finely chopped)
1 tablespoon sugar (i.e. evaporated cane juice)

2 tablespoons each: soy sauce and fresh lime juice
2 tablespoons arrowroot mixed in 2 tablespoons cold water
1 tablespoon coconut oil or olive oil

1. Place mushrooms in blender and blend into powder.
2. In pot, combine mushroom powder, water, parsley, ginger, garlic, and sugar. Bring to simmer over medium heat, stirring occasionally. Reduce heat and simmer, covered, 5 minutes.
3. Allow mixture to cool, then pour through fine-meshed strainer over bowl. Press pulp against strainer with spoon to push liquid through.
4. Combine strained liquid with all remaining ingredients in pot. Bring to simmer over medium heat, stirring frequently until liquid is thick and bubbling. To thicken sauce further, stir in a little more arrowroot-water mixture.
Note: Refrigerate leftovers in glass jar and use within 7 days.
Yield: about 1 cup

Dry Vegetable Broth Seasoning

Sprinkle this tasty seasoning over cooked grains, pasta, and veggies. Or, add to casseroles, soups, dips, and sauces. Or, make Instant 'Chicken' Broth (page 111).

1 cup nutritional yeast flakes
2 teaspoons oat flour (see note)
1 teaspoon each: onion powder, dried parsley, and salt
¾ teaspoon garlic powder
pinch of ground turmeric

1. Place all ingredients in blender and blend into powder.
Note: Store-bought oat flour will yield a much finer texture than homemade oat flour.
Store in airtight container, in a cool spot. Use within 30 days.
Yield: about ¾ cup

'Oyster' Sauce

Subtly sweet and savory, this delicious mushroom-infused sauce will take steamed veggies and cooked grains to a new level.

¾ cup dried shiitake mushrooms (crumbled, about ½ ounce)

1 cup water
1 teaspoon sugar (i.e. evaporated cane juice)

2 tablespoons soy sauce
1 tablespoon arrowroot mixed in 1 tablespoon cold water
1 tablespoon coconut oil or olive oil

1. Place mushrooms in blender and blend into powder.
2. In pot, combine mushroom powder, water, and sugar. Bring to simmer over medium heat, stirring occasionally. Reduce heat and simmer, covered, 5 minutes.
3. Allow mixture to cool 20-30 minutes. Pour mixture through fine-meshed strainer over bowl. Press pulp to push liquid through.
4. Combine strained liquid with all remaining ingredients in pot. Bring to simmer over medium heat, stirring frequently until liquid is thick and bubbling. To thicken sauce further, stir in a little more arrowroot-water mixture.
Note: Refrigerate leftovers in glass jar and use within 7 days.
Yield: about ¾ cup

Roasted Garlic

When roasted, garlic loses its wild, strong character, taking on a buttery flavor and creamy texture. Delicious on crackers and veggies.

1 garlic head (or more, as needed)
1 tablespoon water

1. Preheat toaster oven (or regular oven) to 350°.
2. Break garlic into individual cloves, removing as much loose papery skin as will come off, but leaving cloves unpeeled.
3. Place cloves on sheet of aluminum foil or in small, un-oiled baking dish, and drizzle with water.
4. Fold foil to form packet, or cover baking dish.
5. Bake until cloves are soft, about 1 hour.
6. Remove from oven, let cool. Squeeze to release creamy paste.
Note: Refrigerate leftovers in airtight container. Use within 7 days.

Ponzu (Japanese Sauce)

*A tangy "fishy" sauce that's perfect for dipping sushi
and as a low-sodium alternative to regular soy sauce.*

2 tablespoons each: brown rice vinegar and soy sauce
2 tablespoons mirin (sweet Japanese rice cooking wine)
2 teaspoons ginger juice (see recipe below)
1 teaspoon nori flakes (see recipe below)

1. Combine all ingredients in glass jar and shake to mix thoroughly.
Note: Refrigerate leftovers and use within 7 days.
Yield: about ½ cup

Ginger Juice

*A little ginger juice will add a spirited sweet, peppery flavor
to soups and stir-fries, as well as to spicy cookies and muffins.*

3 two-inch ginger pieces (un-peeled)

1. Wash and pat dry ginger. Grate each piece on a box or hand
grater, using the smallest holes that will allow ginger to come through.
2. Place grated ginger in a small bowl and press with the back of a
spoon to release juice. Or, place ginger in fine-meshed strainer over
a bowl and press with a spoon to release juice. After pressing, take
ginger pulp between your finger tips and squeeze out remaining juice.
Note: Refrigerate and use within 1 day or freeze.
Yield: about 2 tablespoons

Nori Flakes

*Sprinkle these seaweed flakes over salads, grains,
and veggies for an alluring taste of the sea—that some would call "fishy."*

6 sheets toasted nori

1. Tear nori sheets into pieces and place in blender. Blend into flakes,
stopping blender to shake or stir, as necessary.
Note: Store in airtight container, in a cool spot. Use within 30 days.
If un-toasted nori is purchased, it will be necessary to toast it before
using. To toast, place nori on baking sheet and bake 2 minutes at
300°. Nori will turn from purple-black to a bright green color.
Yield: about ½ cup

7 From the Oven

Tofu 'Cutlets'

Plain tofu is easily turned into chewy, "meaty cutlets." They make incredibly good sandwiches. Or, chop into cubes and toss with grains or salad.

16 ounces firm or extra-firm tofu

¼ cup apple cider vinegar or other vinegar
2 tablespoons soy sauce
1 tablespoon toasted sesame oil
1 teaspoon liquid smoke (optional)
2 teaspoons garlic powder
pinch of ground black pepper

1. Preheat oven to 350°.
2. Cut tofu lengthwise into 6-8 slices and arrange in single layer in un-oiled, 8x8" (or similar-sized) glass baking dish.
3. In bowl, combine remaining ingredients and pour over tofu.
4. Bake 30 minutes. Flip tofu and bake 30 minutes, or longer, if crustier and chewier texture desired.

Note: Refrigerate leftovers and use within 7 days.
Yield: 3-4 servings

Tofu 'Mozzarella' Strips

These tasty oven-crisp tofu strips combine a "meaty" texture with mozzarella flavor. Add to salads or eat out of hand.

16 ounces firm or extra-firm tofu

¼ cup fresh lemon juice
3 tablespoons water
2 tablespoons coconut oil (melted) or olive oil
1 tablespoon onion powder
½ teaspoon salt

1. Preheat oven to 350°.
2. Cut tofu lengthwise into 8-10 slices, then again in long strips.
3. Place tofu in un-oiled, 8x8" (or similar-sized) glass baking dish.
4. In bowl, combine remaining ingredients and pour over tofu.
5. Bake 30 minutes. Flip tofu and bake 15 minutes, or longer, if crustier and chewier texture desired.

Note: Refrigerate leftovers and use within 7 days.
Yield: 3-4 servings

Tofu Nuggets

Try these "cheesy" puffy cubes over rice, pasta, or salad. Yum!

16 ounces firm or extra-firm tofu

¼ cup fresh lemon juice or brown rice vinegar
3 tablespoons water
1 tablespoon olive oil or canola oil
1 tablespoon onion powder
½ teaspoon salt

¾ cup nutritional yeast flakes

1. Cut tofu lengthwise into 4 thick slabs. Freeze 4 hours or more.
2. Preheat oven to 350°.
3. Bake frozen tofu 20 minutes in un-oiled baking dish. Let cool.
4. Press each slab between hands to remove excess water.
5. Cut tofu in cubes and transfer to large bowl.
6. Combine remaining ingredients, except yeast flakes, and pour over tofu, tossing until all liquid is absorbed.
7. Sprinkle yeast flakes over tofu and toss to coat.
8. Place tofu in large, oiled glass baking dish and bake 30 minutes, tossing cubes halfway. Bake longer for crispier texture.
Note: Refrigerate leftovers and use within 7 days.
Yield: 3-4 servings

Tempeh Tidbits

Crispy and delectable over grains or salad.

8 ounces tempeh

¼ cup fresh lemon juice
2 tablespoons water
1 tablespoon olive oil or canola oil
1 tablespoon onion powder
½ teaspoon salt

¼ cup flax seed meal (page 29)

1. Preheat oven to 350°.
2. Place tempeh in steamer basket and steam 10 minutes.
3. When tempeh is cool, cut into cubes and place in large bowl.
4. In small bowl combine remaining ingredients, except flax meal, and pour over tempeh cubes. Toss until all liquid is absorbed.
5. Sprinkle flax meal over tempeh and toss to coat.
6. Place tempeh on large, oiled baking sheet and bake 20 minutes. Toss tempeh and bake 15 minutes or longer, for crispier texture.
Note: Refrigerate leftovers and use within 4 days.
Yield: 2-3 servings

Orange Tempeh Strips

These glazed, smoky-sweet strips are amazing over rice or pasta.

8 ounces tempeh (cut in thin strips)

¼ cup frozen orange juice concentrate (thawed)
3 tablespoons apple cider vinegar or other vinegar
2 tablespoons soy sauce
1 tablespoon toasted sesame oil
1 teaspoon garlic powder
½ teaspoon liquid smoke (optional)
pinch of ground black pepper

1. Preheat oven to 325°.
2. Arrange tempeh in un-oiled, 8x8" (or similar-sized) baking dish.
3. Combine remaining ingredients and pour over tempeh.
4. Bake 30 minutes, or longer, if crispier texture desired.
Note: Refrigerate leftovers and use within 4 days.
Yield: 2-3 servings

Tempeh Eggplant 'Parmesan'

This light and luscious version of a classic (cholesterol-laden) dish is rich in protein and fiber, not fat. Enjoy it as often as you wish.

1 medium eggplant

½ cup sun-dried tomatoes (chopped)
1 cup boiling water

12 ounces tempeh (cut in bite-sized pieces)
3 cups pasta sauce
2 cups mushrooms (sliced)
1 medium each: onion and carrot (chopped)
1 tablespoon toasted sesame oil
2 teaspoons each: dried basil, garlic powder, and onion powder
1 teaspoon each: dried oregano and salt

½ cup Sesame 'Parmesan' (page 75)

1. Preheat oven to 400°.
2. Peel eggplant and slice into ¾" rounds. Place eggplant on oiled, baking sheet and bake 10 minutes. Flip and bake 10 minutes more.
3. Place sun-dried tomatoes in bowl, cover with water, and set aside 10-15 minutes.
4. In bowl, combine tempeh with remaining ingredients, except Parmesan. Stir in tomatoes and soaking water.
5. Spread 2 cups of sauce mixture on bottom of oiled 9x13" (or similar-sized) baking dish.
6. Arrange eggplant rounds over sauce mixture. Spread remaining mixture over eggplant.
7. Cover and bake 1 hour. Remove from oven and sprinkle with Sesame 'Parmesan'. Let cool about 10 minutes before serving.
Note: Refrigerate leftovers and use within 4 days.
Yield: 4-6 servings

Oven double-duty is an efficient way to bake. If you're putting a casserole or other main dish in the oven, also bake sweet potatoes or yams, or another dish that calls for the same baking temperature.

Tempeh 'Meatloaf'

This meatless "meatloaf" bursts with flavor, especially of bar-b-q.

1 medium each: onion and carrot (chopped)
¾ cup celery (chopped)

½ cup each: rolled oats and boiling water
¼ cup flax seed meal (page 29)

8 ounces tempeh (chopped)
½ cup Bar-B-Q Sauce (page 87 or store-bought)
2 tablespoons brown rice vinegar or other vinegar
2 teaspoons ground ginger
½ teaspoon each: salt and liquid smoke

½ cup Bar-B-Q Sauce (page 87 or store-bought)

1. Preheat oven to 350°.
2. Place first 3 vegetables in steamer basket and steam 5 minutes.
3. Combine oats, water, and flax in bowl. Let stand 10 minutes.
4. In separate bowl, combine all ingredients, except ½ cup sauce.
5. Pack mixture into oiled loaf pan or pie plate.
6. Spoon remaining ½ cup sauce over loaf top.
7. Bake, uncovered, 1 hour. Let cool 10 minutes before serving.
Note: Refrigerate leftovers and use within 4 days.
Yield: 4 servings

Mold on food requires that the food be discarded. Molds are fungi with deep roots, so forget about trying to cut away the mold. Bread with fuzzy green dots, jelly with a furry surface growth, or fruit with a coin-shaped, soft spot are common mold attacks. On the other hand, some molds are beneficial. Those white, gray, or even black spots or patches on tempeh are natural and harmless. However, mold of another color on tempeh is a sign of spoilage.

Tempeh 'Tuna' Casserole

Tempeh, tofu, and nori lead the way in this creamy, classic casserole.

4 sheets toasted nori

1½ cups uncooked whole-grain noodles

8 ounces tempeh (cut in thin slices)

1 cup mushrooms (sliced)
¾ cup each: celery (sliced) and onion (chopped)

1 recipe Tofu 'Aioli' (page 85)
1 cup green peas (fresh or frozen and thawed)
½ cup non-dairy milk
¼ cup roasted red pepper (chopped) (store-bought)
1 teaspoon garlic powder
½ teaspoon salt

1 cup whole-grain bread crumbs
3 tablespoons nutritional yeast flakes
1 teaspoon paprika

1. Preheat oven to 350°.
2. Tear nori in pieces. Place in blender. Blend into flakes, set aside.
3. Cook noodles in boiling water 8-10 minutes, or until tender. Drain noodles and toss with tempeh.
4. In steamer basket, steam mushrooms, onions, and celery, 5 minutes.
5. Toss steamed ingredients with tempeh and noodles. Stir in next 6 ingredients, mixing well.
6. Pack mixture into oiled 8x8" (or similar-sized) glass baking dish.
7. Combine last 3 ingredients in bowl. Sprinkle over casserole.
8. Cover and bake 60 minutes. Let cool 10 minutes before serving.
Note: Refrigerate leftovers and use within 4 days.
Yield: 4-6 servings

Celery strings are hard to chew and even tougher to digest. To remove these pesky strings, peel the outside edge of each celery stick using a vegetable peeler.

Roasted Soy 'Nuts'

These crisp, chewy little soy nuggets make a delightful, almost addictive, snack.
Toss a handful in a salad for added protein—and crunch!

1¼ cups dried soybeans
6 cups cold water

1 tablespoon coconut oil (melted) or canola oil

¾ teaspoon each: ground cumin and salt
pinch of ground black pepper

1. Pick through beans, discarding any foreign matter. Rinse beans.
2. Place beans in bowl with water. Soak at least 8 hours.
3. Drain and rinse beans thoroughly.
4. Preheat oven to 350°.
5. In bowl, toss beans with oil, then with remaining seasonings.
6. Spread beans on large, oiled baking sheet. Bake 30 minutes, stirring half-way. For crunchier nuts, bake 10 minutes longer.
Note: Refrigerate leftovers and use within 10 days.
Yield: about 2 cups
Variation: For **Roasted Garbo 'Nuts'**, replace dried soybeans with 1¼ cups dried garbanzo beans (chickpeas).

Stuffed Squash

Baked squash with stuffing makes a wonderful alternative to stuffed turkey.

4 small winter squashes (delicata, sweet dumpling, or acorn)

1 recipe Veggie Steam-Fry (page 129)
3 cups cooked buckwheat (page 26)
1 cup cooked black beans or other beans (page 23)
½ cup walnuts or pecans (chopped)
3 tablespoons dark miso mixed in 3 tablespoons water

1. Preheat oven to 350°.
2. Pierce squashes and bake 60 minutes, or until tender.
3. Combine remaining ingredients in large bowl.
4. Cut squashes in half and scoop out seeds and stringy material.
5. Fill halves with stuffing and place in baking dish. Bake 15 minutes.
Note: Refrigerate leftovers and use within 4 days.
Yield: 4-6 servings

Roasted Vegetables

*Roasting sweetens and deepens the flavors—revealing a tasty dimension
not seen with raw or steamed veggies.*

1 medium sweet potato or yam
1 medium parsnip, turnip, or rutabaga
1 medium red onion
1 cup each: broccoli florets and cauliflower florets

1 tablespoon toasted sesame oil
1 tablespoon coconut oil (melted) or olive oil
**½ teaspoon each: curry powder, garlic powder, onion powder, and
  salt**
¼ teaspoon ground black pepper

1. Preheat oven to 425°.
2. Peel vegetables, if desired, then cut into similar-sized chunks.
3. Combine vegetables in bowl and toss with remaining seasonings.
4. Spread vegetables in single layer (if possible) on large, oiled baking sheet or pan and roast 20 minutes, stirring halfway.
Note: Refrigerate leftovers and use within 4 days.
Yield: 3 servings

Roasted Beets

*The rich, earthy flavor of beets is concentrated by roasting.
Its crimson flesh becomes soft, moist, sweet—and tantalizing.*

4 medium beets

1. Preheat oven to 400°.
2. Wash beets, then trim root ends, leaving beet skin un-broken and un-peeled. Wrap each whole beet individually in aluminum foil.
3. Place beets in baking pan and roast 1 hour or until tender.
4. Hold cool beets under cold running water to peel off skin.
5. Cut beets into cubes before serving.
Note: Refrigerate leftovers and use within 4 days.
Yield: 4-6 servings

Roasted Potato Rounds

These morsels emerge from the oven crisp on the outside and tender inside.

4 medium red or yellow potatoes (cut in ½" rounds)

2 tablespoons coconut oil (melted) or canola oil

½ teaspoon each: ground cumin, paprika, and salt
¼ teaspoon ground black pepper

1. Preheat oven to 350°.
2. Place potatoes in steamer basket and steam 8 minutes.
3. In large bowl, toss potatoes with oil, then with next 4 seasonings.
4. Spread potatoes in single layer on large, oiled baking sheet.
5. Bake 45 minutes. Toss potatoes and bake 15 minutes more or until as golden and crisp as desired.
Note: Refrigerate leftovers and use within 4 days.
Yield: 4 servings
Variation: For **Roasted Sweet Potato Rounds**, replace potatoes with sweet potatoes or yams.

Sweet Potato Casserole

A sweet and satisfying side dish. Festive, as well as every day fare.

3 medium sweet potatoes or yams (peeled, cut in small pieces)
1 cup dried apricots or other dried fruit (chopped)
¾ cup walnuts or pecans (chopped)
½ cup each: water and frozen apple juice concentrate (thawed)
1-2 tablespoons coconut oil (melted) (optional)
½ teaspoon each: cinnamon and salt

1. Preheat oven to 350°.
2. Combine all ingredients in bowl and toss.
3. Transfer mixture to oiled casserole dish. Cover and bake 1 hour.
4. Remove from oven and let stand 10 minutes before serving.
Note: Refrigerate leftovers and use within 4 days.
Yield: 4-6 servings

Potatoes with green spots or tint have been overexposed to light. The green is a mild toxin that should be cut away, as should any potato sprouts.

Baked Sweet Potatoes or Yams

The long roast in a hot oven concentrates the sweet flavor in the creamy flesh.

4 medium sweet potatoes or yams

olive oil, flax seed oil, or non-dairy margarine (to taste)
salt (to taste)

1. Preheat oven to 425°.
2. Place sweet potatoes in glass baking dish and pierce with fork.
3. Bake 1¼-1½ hours or until tender when pressed.
4. Cut slit in each and squeeze ends to open. Add seasonings.
Note: Refrigerate leftovers and use within 4 days.
Yield: 4-6 servings

Potato Boats

Crusty on top, soft and steamy inside, these stuffed potatoes are sensational.

3 medium russet (baking) potatoes

4 cups broccoli florets (cut in bite-sized pieces)

1 recipe Tofu 'Sour Cream' (page 86)
1 tablespoon onion powder
½ teaspoon salt
pinch of ground black pepper

1. Preheat oven to 400°.
2. Pierce potatoes with fork and bake 1 hour.
3. Place broccoli in steamer basket and steam 3 minutes. Set aside.
4. Cut potatoes in half lengthwise. Scoop flesh into bowl, leaving ¼-inch-thick shells. Set aside potato shells. Mash flesh until smooth.
5. Stir steamed broccoli, sour cream, and remaining seasonings with mashed potatoes until well combined.
6. Spoon potato mix into each half, making a mound at the centers.
7. Place stuffed potato shells on oiled baking sheet and bake 30 minutes (or broil 5-10 minutes), until golden brown and crusty.
Note: Refrigerate leftovers and use within 4 days.
Yield: 3-6 servings

Navy 'Lasagna'

A sensational lasagna—protein and fiber-rich with only a trace of fat. Mashed navy beans provide the look of melted cheese. And a sprinkle of Sesame 'Parmesan' (page 75) adds a nice touch.

½ cup dried mushrooms (chopped)
½ cup sun-dried tomatoes (chopped)
1¼ cups boiling water

2 cups cooked navy or other white beans (page 23)
½ cup water
½ teaspoon salt

3 cups pasta sauce
1 medium onion (chopped)
1 tablespoon toasted sesame oil
2 teaspoons each: dried basil, garlic powder, and onion powder

6 or 8 whole-grain lasagna noodles

1. Preheat oven to 350°.
2. Place first 3 ingredients in bowl. Set aside 10-15 minutes.
3. In blender, blend next 3 ingredients until thick and pasty.
4. Transfer bean mix to bowl and set aside.
5. In large bowl, combine pasta sauce with next 5 ingredients.
6. Transfer soaked mushrooms, tomatoes, and soak water to bowl of pasta sauce mixture. Combine thoroughly.
7. Spread thin layer of pasta sauce mixture on bottom of oiled 9x13" (or similar-sized) baking dish.
8. Without overlap, layer 3 or 4 uncooked noodles over pasta sauce mixture in baking dish.
9. Spread about ½ of bean paste evenly over noodles.
10. Spread about ½ of pasta sauce mixture evenly over bean paste.
11. Repeat (as in steps 8, 9, & 10 above) with another layer of 3 or 4 uncooked noodles, and cover with remaining bean paste and pasta sauce mixture.
12. Cover and bake 1¼ hours. Let cool 10 minutes before serving.
Note: Refrigerate leftovers and use within 5 days or freeze.
Yield: 4-8 servings
Variation: For **Navy Spinach 'Lasagna'**, combine 4 cups chopped raw spinach (or chopped kale) with pasta sauce mixture and layer as directed above.

Enchiladas

Corn tortillas wrapped around a spicy bean mix and baked until tender. They'll almost melt in your mouth.

1 recipe Chili (page 110)

8 whole-grain corn tortillas (5-6" diameter)

**Veggie Salsa (to taste) (page 80 or store-bought)
green onions (thinly sliced) (to taste)**

1. Preheat oven to 350°.
2. Spread 1 cup chili on bottom of oiled 8x8" (or similar-sized) glass baking dish.
3. Place one tortilla on flat surface and spread about ¼ cup chili across center of tortilla.
4. Roll up tortilla and place seam side down in baking dish. Continue with remaining tortillas in this manner.
5. Pour remaining chili over tortillas. Cover, bake 30 minutes.
Note: Refrigerate leftovers and use within 4 days or freeze.
Yield: 4-8 servings

Chilaquiles

My version of this traditional Mexican entrée is prepared lasagna-style. It's a colorful casserole that sparkles with flavor!

12 whole-grain corn tortillas (5-6" diameter)

1 recipe Chili (page 110)

4 cups raw broccoli florets (chopped)

1 recipe 'Cheddar' Melt (page 73)

1. Preheat oven to 350°.
2. Cut each tortilla into 6 or 8 wedges. Spread half of tortilla wedges on bottom of oiled 8x8" (or similar-sized) glass baking dish.
3. Spoon half of chili over tortillas, then half of broccoli, and half of cheese.
4. Top with remaining tortilla wedges and repeat layering process.
5. Bake uncovered, 30 minutes.
Note: Refrigerate leftovers and use within 4 days or freeze.
Yield: 6-8 servings

Pizza with 'Cheddar'

*A chewy, tasty crust, layered simply with a sauce and several toppings,
is spread with a luscious melted "cheddar cheese." This is the essence of pizza!*

1 recipe Basic Dough (page 29)

½ cup Pizza Sauce (page 87 or store-bought)

1 medium tomato (sliced)
1 cup mushrooms (thinly sliced)
½ cup green onions (thinly sliced)

½ recipe 'Cheddar' Melt (to taste) (page 73)

1-2 tablespoons olive oil or toasted sesame oil (optional)

1. Preheat oven to 400°.
2. Roll out dough to 10-12" circle on floured surface. Prick dough with fork.
3. Transfer dough to oiled baking sheet. Bake 20 minutes, or until crust is just golden.
4. Spread crust with pizza sauce and add layer of tomato slices, mushrooms, and green onions. Top with cheddar melt.
5. Return pizza to oven 10 minutes, or until vegetables are steaming hot. Drizzle with oil, if desired.

Note: Refrigerate leftovers and use within 4 days.

Yield: 3-4 servings

For **Socca Pizza with 'Cheddar'**, replace baked crust with Socca (page 133).

8 Soups & Stews

Red Lentil Dal

A mouth-watering version of the popular Indian stew.

1 medium onion (chopped)

3 medium garlic cloves (finely chopped)
1-2 tablespoons fresh ginger (grated or finely chopped)
½ teaspoon each: ground cumin, curry powder, and salt

1 tablespoon fresh lemon or lime juice
1 recipe Basic Red Lentils (page 24)

1. Lightly oil a non-stick skillet and cook onions, over medium heat, uncovered, stirring often, until onions are soft.
2. Add next 5 ingredients and cook, 1-2 minutes, stirring often.
3. Stir in lemon juice and lentils. Cook briefly to heat thoroughly.
Note: Refrigerate leftovers and use within 5 days.
When chilled overnight, dal hardens. To soften, place dal in small pot with a little water and heat over low heat, stirring often.
Yield: 3-4 servings

Tangy Black Beans

These black beans are sweet, spicy, and robust. They contrast nicely with the sunny corn kernels. Enjoy this zesty saucy dish over hot grains.

2 cups cooked black beans (page 23)
1 medium onion (chopped)
½ cup water
¼ cup corn kernels (fresh or frozen and thawed)
¼ cup fresh lemon juice or apple cider vinegar
1 tablespoon olive oil
1 teaspoon each: ground cumin, garlic powder, and salt
pinch of ground black pepper

2 teaspoons arrowroot mixed in 1 tablespoon cold water

1. Combine all ingredients in pot, except arrowroot mixture. Simmer, covered, until onions are tender, stirring occasionally.
2. Stir arrowroot mixture into simmering beans. Continue simmering, stirring constantly, until sauce thickens, about 15 seconds.
Note: Refrigerate leftovers and use within 5 days.
Yield: 3-4 servings

Split Pea Soup

Thick and hearty, this soup is rich and delicately sweet.

1½ cups dried split peas

4 cups water
1 small onion (chopped)
¾ cup carrot (chopped)
2 tablespoons nutritional yeast flakes (optional)
1 tablespoon toasted sesame oil or olive oil
1 teaspoon each: ground cumin, garlic powder, and salt
½-1 teaspoon liquid smoke (optional)
pinch of ground black pepper

1. Pick through peas, discarding any foreign matter. Rinse peas.
2. In large pot, combine all ingredients. Bring to boil, reduce heat, cover, and simmer 1 hour, or until peas are tender. Stir occasionally.
Note: For creamy soup, let soup cool, then blend until smooth, and reheat. Refrigerate leftovers and use within 7 days or freeze.
Yield: 6-8 servings

'Cream' of Cauliflower Soup

So rich-tasting and creamy. This elegant soup's enchanting flavor is due, in part, from the last-minute addition of miso.

3 cups cauliflower florets (cut in bite-sized pieces)
2 cups each: non-dairy milk and water
2 cups cooked navy or other white beans (page 23)
1 medium onion (chopped)
3 tablespoons cashew butter, almond butter, or tahini
1 tablespoon coconut oil or olive oil
1 tablespoon each: dried chives and dried parsley
1 teaspoon each: dried basil, garlic powder, and salt

3 tablespoons light miso mixed in 3 tablespoons cold water

1. In large pot, combine all ingredients, except miso mixture. Bring to slow boil over medium heat, reduce heat, cover, and simmer 30 minutes. Stir occasionally.
2. Remove soup from heat. Stir in miso mixture and serve.
Note: Refrigerate leftovers and use within 5 days or freeze.
Yield: 6-8 servings
Variation: For **'Cream' of Broccoli Soup**, replace cauliflower florets with broccoli florets.

Boston 'Baked' Beans

Quick, stove-top beans with slow-cooked flavor. It's a sweet and smoky dish.

2 cups cooked navy or pinto beans (page 23)
1 medium onion (chopped)
½ cup blackstrap molasses
2 tablespoons soy sauce
1 tablespoon toasted sesame oil or olive oil
1 tablespoon Dijon-style or stone-ground mustard
1 teaspoon each: garlic powder and liquid smoke (optional)
pinch of ground black pepper

1 tablespoon arrowroot mixed in 1 tablespoon cold water

1. Combine all ingredients in pot, except arrowroot mixture.
2. Bring to simmer over medium heat. Reduce heat, cover, and simmer 15 minutes, or until onions are tender. Stir occasionally.
3. Stir arrowroot mixture into simmering beans. Continue simmering, stirring constantly, until sauce thickens, about 15 seconds.
Note: Refrigerate leftovers and use within 5 days or freeze.
Yield: 3-4 servings

Chili

An irresistible, spirited bean fusion—no matter how you serve it.

2 cups cooked black, pinto, or kidney beans (page 23)
2 cups Veggie Salsa (page 80 or store-bought)
¾ cup corn kernels (fresh or frozen and thawed)
¾ cup carrot (chopped)
1 small onion (chopped)
1 tablespoon chili powder
1 teaspoon each: ground cumin, garlic powder, onion powder, salt, and liquid smoke (optional)
½ teaspoon ground cayenne pepper (optional)
pinch of ground black pepper

1. In a large pot, combine all ingredients.
2. Bring to simmer over medium heat. Reduce heat, cover, and simmer 15 minutes, or until vegetables are tender. Stir occasionally.
Note: Refrigerate leftovers and use within 5 days or freeze.
Yield: 4-6 servings
Variation: For **Tempeh Chili**, add 8 ounces tempeh (cubed) to step 1. Just before serving, stir in 3 tablespoons dark miso mixed in 3 tablespoons water, and 2 medium tomatoes (chopped).

Beans & Greens Soup

Beans and greens make an unbeatable combination!
The final 3 ingredients give this soup a depth of flavor that is astounding.

6 cups kale (finely chopped)
4 cups water
2 cups cooked navy or other beans (page 23)
2 cups cauliflower florets (chopped)
1 medium each: carrot and onion (chopped)
1 tablespoon toasted sesame oil or olive oil
2 teaspoons dried parsley
1 teaspoon each: garlic powder and salt

3 tablespoons dark miso mixed in 3 tablespoons cold water
2 tablespoons fresh lemon juice
2 tablespoons nutritional yeast flakes

1. In large pot, combine all ingredients, except miso, lemon juice, and nutritional yeast. Bring to boil over medium-high heat, reduce heat, cover, and simmer 30 minutes. Stir occasionally.

2. Just before serving, stir in miso, lemon juice, and yeast flakes.

Note: Refrigerate leftovers and use within 5 days or freeze.

Yield: 4-6 servings

Variation: Replace kale with chopped collard greens or bok choy.

For **Red Lentils & Greens Soup**, replace cooked beans with 2 cups cooked red lentils (page 24).

Instant 'Chicken' Broth

No need for pre-made liquid stocks. Flavor-rich with a golden hue,
this wholesome broth is ready whenever you need it.

2 cups water

2 tablespoons Dry Vegetable Broth Seasoning (page 90)

1. Place water in medium pot and whisk in seasoning. Bring to boil, reduce heat and simmer 1 minute.

Yield: 2 cups

Corn Chowder

A thick, rich-tasting soup bursting with the flavors and textures of corn and sweet potato. It's incredibly good using Coconut Milk (page 35).

2 cups each: water and non-dairy milk
1 cup cooked navy or other beans (page 23)
1 medium onion (chopped)
1 medium sweet potato or yam (peeled and chopped)
½ cup celery (chopped)
½ cup green onions (thinly sliced)
2 tablespoons olive oil or toasted sesame oil
2 tablespoons dried parsley
2 teaspoons garlic powder
1 teaspoon each: paprika, dried thyme, and salt
pinch of ground black pepper

2 cups corn kernels (fresh or frozen and thawed)

2 tablespoons light miso mixed in 2 tablespoons cold water

1. Combine all ingredients, except corn and miso, in large pot. Bring to slow boil on medium heat, reduce heat, cover, and simmer 20 minutes, or until vegetables are tender. Stir occasionally.
2. Add corn and simmer several minutes to heat corn thoroughly.
3. Remove chowder from heat. Stir in miso mixture and serve.
Note: Refrigerate leftovers and use within 5 days.
Yield: 4-6 servings
Variation: For richer, creamier chowder, replace water with non-dairy milk. For deeper flavor, replace light miso with dark miso.

Cup of Miso Soup

An instant soup with an astounding depth of flavors.

1 tablespoon nutritional yeast flakes
2-3 teaspoons light or dark miso
1 sheet toasted nori (torn in small pieces)
1 teaspoon fresh lemon juice (optional)

1 cup boiling water

1. Place first 4 ingredients in cup.
2. Stir in a little water, mixing thoroughly. Add remaining water.
Yield: 1 serving

Tofu 'Chicken' Noodle Soup

*This tofu stand-in has all the flavor, as well as legendary
healing powers, of regular chicken soup.*

½ cup dried yellow split peas

7 cups water
1 small onion (chopped)
½ cup each: carrots (chopped) and celery (chopped)
2 tablespoons nutritional yeast flakes
1 tablespoon olive oil or canola oil
1 tablespoon dried parsley
1 teaspoon each: garlic powder and salt
¼ teaspoon ground turmeric

4-6 Tofu 'Cutlets' (page 94) or 8 ounces firm or extra-firm tofu

1 cup whole-grain noodles (about 3 ounces)

½ cup green peas (fresh or frozen and thawed)

1. Pick through yellow split peas, discarding any foreign matter.
Rinse peas.
2. In pot, combine all ingredients, except tofu, noodles, and green
peas. Bring to boil, over medium-high heat, reduce heat, cover, and
simmer 45 minutes. Stir occasionally.
3. In separate pot, cook noodles in boiling water, until just tender,
8-10 minutes. Drain noodles, rinse, and set aside.
4. Chop tofu into small cubes and add with noodles to soup pot.
Simmer 10 minutes longer.
5. Add green peas and simmer several minutes longer.
Note: Refrigerate leftovers and use within 5 days or freeze.
Yield: 4-6 servings

Miso Tortilla Soup

A creamy and corny tortilla soup. Quick and satisfying.

4 whole-grain corn tortillas (5 or 6" diameter)
3 cups water
2 tablespoons nutritional yeast flakes
1 teaspoon each: dried parsley and onion powder

1 cup corn kernels (fresh or frozen and thawed)

2-3 tablespoons dark miso mixed in 2-3 tablespoons water
2 teaspoons olive oil

1. Rip tortillas in pieces and combine with next 4 ingredients in pot.
2. Bring to slow boil over medium heat, reduce heat, cover and simmer several minutes, stirring often.
3. Add corn and heat briefly. Stir in miso and oil and serve.
Note: Refrigerate leftovers and use within 5 days.
Yield: 2-3 servings
Variation: Tear 2 sheets of toasted nori and add to pot with corn.

Root Chowder

A hearty stew, richly-flavored and distinctively sweet.

2 cups each: water and non-dairy milk
1 medium each: carrot (chopped) and onion (chopped)
1 medium sweet potato or yam (peeled and chopped)
1 cup parsnips (chopped)
¼ cup dried mushrooms (crumbled) (optional)
2 tablespoons each: coconut oil or olive oil and dried parsley
1 teaspoon each: garlic and onion powder, dried basil, and salt
½ teaspoon ground cayenne pepper

3 cups broccoli florets (cut in bite-sized pieces)
2 cups corn kernels (fresh or frozen and thawed)

3 tablespoons dark miso mixed in 3 tablespoons cold water

1. In large pot, combine all ingredients, except broccoli, corn, and miso. Bring to slow boil on medium heat, reduce heat, cover, and simmer 20 minutes.
2. Add broccoli and corn. Simmer 5 minutes more.
3. Remove chowder from heat. Stir in miso mixture.
Note: Refrigerate leftovers and use within 5 days or freeze.
Yield: 4-6 servings

9 Wraps, Patties, & Sandwiches

Falafel

These baked garbanzo bean balls are delicious stuffed into whole-grain pita and drenched with Tofu 'Aioli' (page 85).

1¼ cups garbanzo bean flour
¼ cup flax seed meal (page 29)
2 tablespoons dried parsley
1½ teaspoons each: garlic powder and onion powder
½ teaspoon salt

½ cup water
2 tablespoons each: fresh lemon juice and tahini
1 tablespoon toasted sesame oil

1 small onion (finely chopped)

1. Preheat oven to 350°.
2. In bowl, combine first 6 dry ingredients.
3. In separate bowl, whisk next 4 wet ingredients.
4. Stir wet and dry ingredients. Mix in onions. Form a stiff dough.
5. Moisten hands and form dough into 1" diameter balls.
6. Bake balls on oiled baking sheet for 35 minutes, flipping halfway.
Note: Refrigerate leftovers and use within 5 days.
Yield: 4-5 servings

Bean Burritos

Burritos are quick and easy—to make and to grab-and-go!

1 recipe Chili (page 110)
6 large whole-grain tortillas

1. Preheat oven to 325°.
2. Place one tortilla on flat surface and spread about ⅔ cup hot bean mixture across center of tortilla.
3. Roll up tortilla and place in oiled 9x13" (or similar-sized) baking dish. Repeat process with remaining tortillas. Cover, bake 30 minutes.
Note: Refrigerate leftovers and use within 5 days or freeze.
Yield: 3-6 servings
Variation: Burritos can be served without baking. Warm tortillas in oven, then spread hot bean mixture on each tortilla. Top with layer of fresh vegetables, such as shredded lettuce, chopped cucumber, sliced avocado, and chopped tomato. Roll and serve.

Black Bean Burgers

Beans, whole grains, and seeds combine to make hearty, crusty burgers.

1 small onion (finely chopped)
¼ cup water

2 cups cooked black beans (page 23)

1½ cups cooked buckwheat (page 26)
¼ cup roasted sunflower seed meal (page 30)
¼ cup flax seed meal (page 29)
2 tablespoons dried parsley
1 teaspoon each: garlic powder, onion powder, and dried thyme
½ teaspoon salt
pinch of ground black pepper

2 tablespoons each: fresh lemon juice and soy sauce
1 teaspoon liquid smoke

1. Preheat oven to 350°.
2. Place onions and water in pot. Bring to boil over medium heat, reduce heat, cover and simmer until onions are soft, about 5 minutes.
3. Mash beans in bowl. Stir in all ingredients, except lemon juice, soy sauce, and liquid smoke.
4. In separate bowl, combine last 3 ingredients. Stir into bean mixture, mixing well.
5. Moisten hands and form mixture into 3" burgers.
6. Bake burgers on oiled baking sheet for 30 minutes, flipping burgers halfway.

Note: To cook burgers in skillet, lightly oil a non-stick skillet and cook burgers over medium heat 5 minutes on each side or until as browned as desired.

Refrigerate leftovers and use within 5 days or freeze.

Yield: 4-6 servings

Freezing Fresh Herbs: Put a tablespoon of chopped herbs into the bottom of each compartment of an ice cube tray. Cover with water and freeze. Store in an airtight container. To use, add a cube or two to simmering soups, stews, or stir-fries.

Veggie Garbo Burgers

Colorful and festive, these chewy, delicious veggie burgers are outstanding!

1½ cups garbanzo bean flour
¼ cup flax seed meal (page 29)
2 tablespoons dried parsley
1 teaspoon onion powder
½ teaspoon each: garlic powder and salt

¼ cup water
2 tablespoons soy sauce
2 tablespoons fresh lemon juice or apple cider vinegar
1 tablespoon toasted sesame oil
1 teaspoon liquid smoke (optional)

1 medium carrot (grated)
1 small onion (finely chopped)
2 celery stalks (finely chopped)
¼ cup roasted red pepper (finely chopped) (store-bought)

1. Preheat oven to 350°.
2. Combine first 6 dry ingredients in bowl.
3. In separate bowl, combine next 5 wet ingredients. Add vegetables and toss.
4. Add vegetable mixture to dry ingredients and combine.
5. Moisten hands and form mixture into 3" patties.
6. Bake burgers on oiled baking sheet for 40 minutes, flipping burgers halfway.

Note: To cook burgers in skillet, lightly oil a non-stick skillet and cook burgers over medium heat 5 minutes on each side or until as browned as desired.

Refrigerate leftovers and use within 5 days or freeze.

Yield: 4-6 servings

Spices and herbs are often considered one and the same by many people. While these everyday seasonings may mingle side by side in your cupboard, they are not the same. Spices are pungent or aromatic, and are obtained from dry, hard parts of plants, such as the seeds, berries, bark, or stems. Herbs are fragrant, and made from the leaves of various plants and shrubs.

Broccoli Sweet Potato Patties

Broccoli and sweet potatoes make these patties sweet and colorful.

2 medium sweet potatoes or yams (peeled and cut in chunks)

4 cups broccoli florets (cut in bite-sized pieces)

¼ cup flax seed meal (page 29)
2 tablespoons coconut oil (optional)
1 teaspoon onion powder
½ teaspoon each: garlic powder and salt

1. Preheat oven to 350°.
2. Steam potatoes in steamer basket 10 minutes. Add broccoli and steam 5 minutes more, or until both potatoes and broccoli are tender.
3. Transfer potatoes and broccoli to bowl and combine with remaining ingredients, mashing and mixing well. Let cool to touch.
4. Moisten hands and form mixture into 3" patties.
5. Bake patties on oiled, baking sheet, 40 minutes, flipping halfway.
Note: Refrigerate leftovers and use within 4 days or freeze.
Yield: 3-4 servings

Potato Patties

Golden little potato cakes that are crusty outside, tender inside. Yum!

3 medium potatoes (cut in chunks)

½ cup onions (finely chopped)
3 tablespoons flax seed meal (page 29)
2 tablespoons olive oil or coconut oil
1 teaspoon each: garlic powder and onion powder
½ teaspoon salt
pinch of ground black pepper

1. Preheat oven to 350°.
2. Place potatoes in steamer basket and steam 15 minutes.
3. Transfer potatoes to bowl. Mash potatoes and stir in remaining ingredients. Let cool to touch.
4. Moisten hands and form mixture into 3" patties.
5. Bake patties on oiled baking sheet, 30 minutes, flipping halfway.
Note: Refrigerate leftovers and use within 5 days or freeze.
Yield: 3-4 servings

Tempeh Breakfast 'Sausages'

Snappy tempeh "sausages" packed with wholesome soy protein and flavor.

8 ounces tempeh (cut in several pieces)

¼ cup water
2 tablespoons each: fresh lemon juice, soy sauce, and cashew butter
½ teaspoon liquid smoke (optional)

¼ cup flax seed meal (page 29)
1 teaspoon each: garlic powder, onion powder, and dried thyme
½ teaspoon each: dried oregano and dried sage
pinch of ground black pepper

1. Preheat oven to 350°.
2. Place tempeh in steamer basket and steam 15 minutes.
3. Remove tempeh from steamer and let cool to touch.
4. Grate or mash tempeh in bowl.
5. In separate bowl, combine water and next 4 wet ingredients. Add to tempeh and toss.
6. Add remaining dry ingredients to tempeh mixture and mix well.
7. Moisten hands and form mixture into 2" flat patties.
8. Bake patties on oiled baking sheet, 25 minutes, flipping halfway.

Note: To cook patties in skillet, lightly oil a non-stick skillet and cook patties over medium heat 3-4 minutes on each side or until as browned as desired.

Refrigerate leftovers and use within 4 days or freeze.

Yield: 3-4 servings

Variation: For **Tempeh 'Meatballs'**, continue with steps 1-6 above, but in step 7 shape mixture into 16-20 balls (1-1½" diameter). Bake a total of 20 minutes, flipping halfway. Serve with pasta and sauce.

Dried **herbs** are more potent than fresh ones, because as the leaves are dried, flavorful oils remain and concentrate. To replace fresh herbs with dried, use about ⅓ as much dried as you would the fresh. For best flavor, add dried herbs at the start of cooking (gives herbs time to release their flavors) or add fresh herbs near the end of cooking (protects fresh herbs from losing their delicate flavors).

Tempeh 'Fajitas'

Sautéed veggies and glazed tempeh rolled up in hearty whole-grain tortillas.

1 recipe Veggie Steam-Fry (page 129)
1 recipe Orange Tempeh Strips (page 96)

6 large whole-grain tortillas

1. Evenly divide vegetables and tempeh strips in center of each tortilla (see note below).
2. Fold bottom of each tortilla up about half-way, then fold two sides in to create a hand-sized edible container. Or, roll up in a simple burrito-style.

Note: To make tortillas soft and pliable, stack tortillas on foil and wrap up tightly. Heat in oven at 350° about 5 minutes until steamy. Or, briefly heat one tortilla at a time in a hot dry skillet. Then, stack on a plate and cover with a cloth napkin or towel to keep warm.

Refrigerate leftovers and use within 4 days or freeze.

Yield: 3-6 servings

Tempeh 'Reuben' Sandwiches

This wholesome version of a traditional Reuben sandwich, popular on the New York deli scene, is made with tempeh. Just needs a side of pickles.

2½ cups red or green cabbage (shredded)
1 medium onion (thinly sliced)
2 tablespoons fresh lemon juice

6 slices whole-grain bread (toasted, if desired)

Thousand Island Dressing (to taste) (page 66)

1 recipe Orange Tempeh Strips (page 96)

1. Lightly oil a non-stick skillet and cook all ingredients, over medium heat, covered, until vegetables are as tender as desired. Stir frequently, adding a little water if vegetables are sticking. Set aside.
2. Lay bread slices on flat surface and spread with dressing.
3. Evenly divide tempeh strips over 3 bread slices. Top each with equal portions of cabbage and onion mixture.
4. Close up sandwiches with remaining bread slices.

Yield: 3 sandwiches

Tempeh Roll-Ups

Crispy, golden wraps revealing savory tempeh with each bite.
Perfect with mustard, ketchup, or other tangy sauce.

8 ounces tempeh

¼ cup brown rice vinegar or fresh lemon juice
1 tablespoon olive oil or coconut oil (melted)
2 teaspoons onion powder
½ teaspoon salt

¼ cup flax seed meal (page 29)

½ recipe Basic Dough (page 29)

1. Preheat oven to 400°.
2. Place tempeh in steamer basket, and steam 15 minutes.
3. Remove tempeh from steamer and let cool to touch.
4. Cut tempeh into strips and gently toss with next 4 ingredients in bowl. Add flax meal and toss. Set aside.
5. Transfer dough ball to floured surface. Cut ball into halves. Roll out each to 10" circle.
6. Cut each circle into 8 wedges. Lay one or more tempeh strips on each wedge base and roll to tip to enclose tempeh.
7. Place wraps on oiled baking sheet and bake 25 minutes or until as golden as desired.
Note: Refrigerate leftovers and use within 4 days or freeze.
Yield: 4-6 servings
Variation: After rolling out dough circles, spread each with mustard before cutting into wedges.

Spices are typically available in both whole and ground forms. If you purchase whole, you'll need a small spice grinder. Ground spices are convenient and do offer reasonable flavor. However, they lose their aroma and flavor quickly. It's best to store them in a cool, dark spot and to use them up within 6 months of purchase (write the date on the jar or lid when you first buy it). And, don't shake or pour the spice (or herb) jar directly into a simmering pot. Steam will get into the jar and get your seasonings damp and moldy.

'Sushi'

Making sushi at home is a breeze. No special equipment needed.
Rice is seasoned, then spread on a sheet of nori seaweed.
A filling is added, then a quick roll-up and slice. That's it!

1¼ cups uncooked short-grain brown rice
2½ cups water

½ cup brown rice vinegar or apple cider vinegar
3 tablespoons sugar (i.e. evaporated cane juice)
1 teaspoon salt

6 sheets toasted nori

Suggested fillings: steamed carrot, daikon radish, or zucchini sticks; steamed asparagus; cucumber or avocado strips; chopped nuts or sesame seeds; Tofu 'Cutlet' strips (page 94)

1. Pick through rice, discarding any foreign matter. Rinse rice.
2. In pot, combine rice and water. Bring to boil over medium-high heat, reduce heat, cover, and simmer 40 minutes or until water is absorbed. Remove pot from heat.
3. Transfer hot rice to bowl and combine with vinegar, sugar, and salt. Allow rice to cool to a warm temperature.
4. Place one nori sheet on clean surface.
5. With wet spoon, spread ½ cup rice in thin layer over nori sheet, leaving 1½" strip along top edge bare without rice.
6. Arrange filling ingredients of your choice over rice, about 1½" from bottom edge of nori sheet.
7. Moisten rice-free top strip with dab of water. With wet fingers of both hands, start at rice-filled bottom edge and roll up nori sheet as tight as possible, using the wet strip on top to seal the roll closed.
8. Set aside rolled nori, seam side down, and repeat process with remaining ingredients. Allow finished sushi rolls to rest at least 15 minutes to soften before slicing.
9. Use sharp, moistened, serrated knife to cut each roll into pieces.
Note: Refrigerate leftovers and use within 4 days.
Yield: 4-6 servings
Variation: Spread thin layer (about ½ teaspoon) of wasabi paste, mustard, or other spicy paste along with filling in step 6.

'Welsh Rabbit' (cheddar toast)

The British occasionally enjoy a meal of melted cheddar cheese over toast called Welsh Rabbit. My cholesterol-free, wholesome version is a luxuriant, open-faced sandwich with big, bold flavors.

4 slices whole-grain bread (toasted, if desired)

2 medium tomatoes (sliced)
1 medium avocado (sliced) (optional)

1 recipe 'Cheddar' Melt (page 73)

1. Lay bread slices on flat surface and top each with tomato and avocado slices.
2. Spoon hot 'Cheddar' Melt over sliced tomato and avocado.
Note: Refrigerate leftovers and use within 1 day.
Yield: 4 open-faced sandwiches
Variation: Replace avocado with sliced cucumber or steamed broccoli florets. Sprinkle chopped parsley or cilantro over 'Cheddar' Melt before serving.

Bean 'Bruschetta' with Collards

My make-over of this traditional Italian garlic bread combines hearty whole-grain bread with a tasty mix of beans and greens.

1½ cups cooked navy beans (page 23)
1 tablespoon olive oil or flax seed oil
2 medium garlic cloves (finely chopped) or 1 teaspoon powder
1 teaspoon dried thyme
¼ teaspoon salt
pinch of ground black pepper

1 recipe Collard 'Spaghetti' (page 57)

4 slices whole-grain bread (toasted, if desired)

1. Place first 6 ingredients in bowl and mash until smooth.
2. Lay bread slices on flat surface. Evenly spread bean mixture on each bread slice, then top with greens.
Note: Refrigerate leftovers and use within 1 day.
Yield: 4 open-faced sandwiches

10 From the Skillet

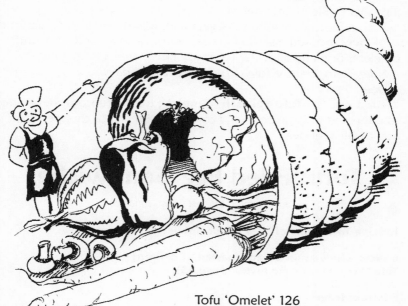

Tofu 'Omelet'

Tofu is the shining star here in creating a tasty, tender, and puffy "omelet" without a drop of cholesterol or saturated animal fat.

16 ounces firm or extra-firm tofu

1 cup water
¾ teaspoon salt
¼ teaspoon ground turmeric

1. Cut tofu into several pieces and place in blender with remaining ingredients. Blend until smooth.
2. Transfer tofu mixture to large, oiled, non-stick skillet. Cover, and cook over medium heat 25 minutes. Remove cover and cook until omelet is firm and all water has evaporated, about 15 minutes.
Note: Refrigerate leftovers and use within 4 days.
Yield: 3 servings
Variation: For **Tofu Spinach 'Omelet'**, transfer uncooked, blended tofu mixture to large bowl and combine with 4 cups chopped spinach. Cook as above.

Tofu 'Fried Egg' Sandwiches

An amazing eggless "egg" sandwich.

1 recipe Tofu 'Omelet' (see recipe above)

6 slices whole-grain bread (toasted, if desired)
Tofu 'Mayonnaise' (to taste) (page 85)

6 lettuce leaves
2 medium tomatoes (sliced)

1. Cut prepared omelet into 3 wedges and set aside.
2. Lay bread slices on flat surface and spread with mayonnaise.
3. Place omelet wedges over 3 bread slices. Top each with lettuce and tomato. Close up sandwiches with remaining bread slices.
Yield: 3 servings

Tofu Scrambled 'Eggs' & Greens

Scrambled "eggs" that are soft, moist, and packed with nourishing greens.

16 ounces firm or extra-firm tofu

6 cups collard greens or kale (stemmed and chopped)
1 medium onion (chopped)

½ cup water
1 tablespoon fresh lemon juice
1 teaspoon liquid smoke (optional)
1 teaspoon garlic powder
½ teaspoon salt
¼ teaspoon ground turmeric
pinch of ground black pepper

1 recipe Tofu 'Sour Cream' (page 86), Tofu 'Aioli' (page 85), or salsa (page 80 or store-bought)

1. Place tofu in skillet and mash. Add chopped greens and onions.
2. Stir in remaining ingredients, except sour cream, aioli, or salsa. Bring to simmer over medium heat, cover, and cook 10 minutes, stirring occasionally.
3. Remove cover and continue simmering until water in skillet has evaporated and tofu is light and fluffy, stirring occasionally.
4. Toss with sour cream, aioli, or salsa.
Note: Refrigerate leftovers and use within 4 days.
Yield: 3-4 servings

Storing Greens: While growing in the fields and even after being picked, such greens as leaf lettuce, spinach, collards, kale, and bok choy, "breathe." Refrigerating and storing these greens in plastic will reduce their rate of respiration (breathing). This slows down their decay and keeps them fresh longer. At home, remove any bands or ties from the greens. Then, roll up unwashed greens like a sleeping bag between paper towels (this will keep the greens neither too wet nor too dry). Place greens in a plastic bag and store in the refrigerator until needed, up to 5 days.

Tofu 'Egg Fried' Rice

*This wholesome version of the popular Asian dish eliminates
the refined rice and animal protein. Absolutely delicious!*

16 ounces firm or extra-firm tofu

¼ cup water
1 cup mushrooms (sliced)
1 teaspoon liquid smoke (optional)
½ teaspoon salt
¼ teaspoon ground turmeric

3 cups cooked brown rice (page 25)
3 tablespoons soy sauce
2 tablespoons toasted sesame oil

½ cup green onions (sliced)
¼ cup roasted almonds or cashews (chopped) (page 30)

1. Place tofu in skillet and mash. Add water and next 4 ingredients
and combine. Bring to simmer over medium heat, reduce heat, cover
and cook about 5 minutes, stirring occasionally.

2. Remove cover and continue simmering until water in skillet has
evaporated and tofu is light and fluffy, stirring occasionally.

3. Add rice, soy sauce, and oil to the skillet with the cooked tofu
and continue cooking until all ingredients are heated thoroughly.

4. Just before serving, stir in green onions and nuts.

Note: Refrigerate leftovers and use within 4 days.

Yield: 4 servings

Variation: Replace cooked rice with equal amount of cooked buckwheat (page 26) or quinoa (page 26). Just before serving stir
in medium grated carrot and ½ cup chopped roasted red pepper
(store-bought).

> **Raw mushrooms** contain toxic compounds (hydrazines) which are
> destroyed in cooking. Therefore, the use of fresh, raw mushrooms in
> salads or other uncooked dishes is not recommended.

Veggie Steam-Fry

So flavorful and colorful, this simple steam-fry relies mostly on the moisture escaping from the veggies to do the cooking. Serve over grains or pasta.

4 cups broccoli florets (cut in bite-sized pieces)
2 cups cauliflower florets (cut in bite-sized pieces)
2 medium carrots (sliced diagonally)
1 medium bell pepper (halved, seeded, and sliced)
1 medium red onion (halved and sliced)
1 teaspoon each: ground cumin, curry powder, and garlic powder
½ teaspoon salt

1. Lightly oil a non-stick skillet and cook all ingredients, over medium heat, covered, until vegetables are as tender as desired. Stir frequently, adding a little water if vegetables are sticking.

Note: Refrigerate leftovers and use within 4 days.

Yield: 3-4 servings

Variation: Add any of the following sliced vegetables to step 1: mushrooms, zucchini, or parsnips.

Pasta 'Primavera'

This delectable take on a traditional Italian favorite combines lots of colorful veggies and whole-grain noodles with a tasty Asian-style sauce.

3 cups uncooked whole-grain noodles (about 8 ounces)

1 tablespoon olive oil, canola oil, or coconut oil
½ teaspoon salt

1 recipe Veggie Steam-Fry (see recipe above)

to taste: Thai Sauce (page 90), Peanut Sauce (page 89), or Teriyaki Sauce (page 88)

1. Cook noodles in boiling water 8-10 minutes, or until tender. Drain and return noodles to pot.

2. Toss noodles with oil and salt.

3. Add noodles to vegetables. Heat briefly, then toss with sauce of choice.

Note: Refrigerate leftovers and use within 4 days.

Yield: 4-6 servings

Tempeh 'Stroganoff'

Tempeh makes an outstanding meat-replacer in this classic 19th century Russian dish. It's a creamy treat of unique flavors and textures.

8 ounces tempeh (cut in ½" cubes)
1 medium onion (chopped)
1 cup mushrooms (sliced)
½ cup water
3 tablespoons soy sauce
1 tablespoon toasted sesame oil
1 teaspoon each: garlic powder, onion powder, and dried thyme

3 cups uncooked whole-grain noodles (about 8 ounces)

1 tablespoon olive oil, canola oil, or coconut oil
½ teaspoon salt

1 recipe Tofu 'Sour Cream' (page 86) or Tofu 'Aioli' (page 85)

1. In skillet, combine first 9 ingredients. Bring to simmer over medium heat, reduce heat, cover, and cook 15 minutes.
2. Cook noodles in boiling water 8-10 minutes, or until tender. Drain and return noodles to pot.
3. Toss noodles with oil and salt.
4. Combine noodles with cooked tempeh mixture in skillet. Heat briefly, then toss with sauce of choice.
Note: Refrigerate leftovers and use within 4 days.
Yield: 4 servings

Chopping and slicing onions have brought tears to many. While folk tales abound with techniques to reduce tearing, the most effective could be as simple as just chilling the onion first. Place the onion in the freezer for about 1 hour before cutting into it. Some truly onion-sensitive souls have resorted to wearing goggles while chopping onions, or even to using a food processor for a single onion.

Tempeh Hash

Tempeh makes this meatless spin on traditional hash quite hearty.
This "supper in a skillet" makes an absolutely delicious breakfast or lunch, too.

2 medium yellow or red potatoes (cut in ½" cubes)
1 medium onion (chopped)
1 cup mushrooms (sliced)
2 medium garlic cloves (finely chopped) or 1 teaspoon powder
1-2 tablespoons fresh ginger (grated) (optional)
1 tablespoon onion powder
½ teaspoon salt

1 recipe Tempeh Tidbits (page 96)

1. Lightly oil non-stick skillet and place over medium heat. Add all ingredients, except tempeh, and cook, covered, stirring often until vegetables are tender, 8-10 minutes.
2. Add tempeh to skillet and cook, uncovered, stirring often until tempeh is heated thoroughly.
Note: Replace Tempeh Tidbits with 8 ounces cubed tempeh, steamed 15 minutes in steamer basket.
Refrigerate leftovers and use within 4 days.
Yield: 3-4 servings

'Sourdough' Skillet Bread

These tangy, yeast-free flat breads are a snap to make.
Serve them plain, or lightly brushed with olive, flax, or melted coconut oil.

1 recipe Basic 'Sourdough' (page 29)

1. Place dough ball on floured surface. Cut ball in half, then in half again, and continue, until there are 8 equal-sized balls.
2. On floured surface, roll each ball to 5" circle, about ¼" thick.
3. Preheat an un-oiled, non-stick skillet over medium heat. Skillet is ready when a drop of water "dances" over the surface.
4. Place 2 or 3 flat breads at a time in skillet and cook until lightly browned, about 10 minutes. Flip and cook other sides until as golden as desired.
Note: Refrigerate leftovers and use within 6 days.
Yield: 4-8 servings

'Egg Foo Yong'

Tofu and garbanzo bean flour combine to create this large savory pancake with a crusty exterior and creamy center.

1½ cups water
8 ounces firm or extra-firm tofu
¾ cup garbanzo bean flour
1 tablespoon onion powder
1 teaspoon garlic powder
½ teaspoon salt
¼ teaspoon ground turmeric
pinch of ground black pepper

2 cups bok choy or cabbage (shredded)
¾ cup carrot (grated)
½ cup green onions (thinly sliced)

'Oyster' Sauce (to taste) (page 91)

1. Preheat oven to 350°.
2. Place first 8 ingredients in blender and blend until smooth.
3. Combine remaining 3 vegetables in bowl. Stir in blender mixture.
4. Lightly oil a non-stick skillet and place over medium heat. Skillet is ready when a drop of water "dances" over the surface.
5. Pour batter in skillet. Cover and cook 15 minutes. Remove cover and cook until pancake bottom is golden and firm, about 10 minutes.
6. Slide pancake out onto oiled baking sheet and bake 30 minutes.
7. Transfer pancake to platter and drizzle with sauce. Slice into wedges or other shapes and serve.

Note: Refrigerate leftovers and use within 5 days.
Yield: 2-3 servings

Socca

No one will guess this savory, French pancake is made from beans!
Crisp outside, tender inside, and with a delightful nutty flavor.

1½ cups garbanzo bean flour
¼ cup flax seed meal (page 29)
1 tablespoon onion powder
1 teaspoon caraway seeds (optional)
¾ teaspoon salt

1½ cups water
¼ cup fresh lemon juice

olive oil or flax seed oil (to taste)
salt (to taste)

1. Preheat oven to 375°.
2. Combine first 5 dry ingredients in bowl.
3. Combine water and lemon juice and stir into bowl of dry ingredients, whisking until batter is smooth and thick.
4. Lightly oil a non-stick skillet and place over medium heat. Skillet is ready when a drop of water "dances" over the surface.
5. Pour batter in skillet. Cook until pancake bottom is golden brown and firm, about 10 minutes.
6. Slide pancake out onto oiled baking sheet and bake 30 minutes.
7. Transfer pancake to platter and drizzle with oil and salt. Or, season with other sauce, if desired.
Note: For crispier pancake, flip pancake after initial 30 minutes baking, and bake 15 minutes more.
Refrigerate leftovers and use within 5 days.
Yield: 4-5 servings
Variation: For "cheesy" flavor, add 2-3 tablespoons nutritional yeast flakes to bowl of dry ingredients in step 2.
For **Socca with Greek Salad Topping**, combine in bowl, 1 cup each: sliced cucumber, tomato, green onions, and grated 'Mozzarella Nut Cheese' (page 68). Toss with 1 tablespoon olive oil, 2 tablespoons fresh lemon juice, ¼ teaspoon salt, and pinch of ground black pepper. Spoon salad over socca.

Dosas

Traditional dosas are large South Indian,
pancake-like breads made with refined flour.
These crisp dosas are made wholesome with brown rice and lentils.

½ cup dried red lentils
½ cup uncooked short-grain brown rice
2 cups water

1 cup water
3 tablespoons each: fresh lemon juice and cashew butter
2 teaspoons onion powder
¼ teaspoon salt

½ cup fresh parsley (finely chopped) (optional)

1. Pick through lentils and rice and remove any foreign matter. Rinse lentils and rice.

2. Place lentils, rice, and 2 cups water in bowl. Cover and refrigerate overnight (at least 8 hours).

3. Drain and rinse soaked lentils and rice. Place in blender with 1 cup fresh water and next 4 ingredients, and blend until smooth, adding more water, as necessary, for smooth consistency.

4. Transfer mixture to bowl and stir in parsley, if using.

5. Preheat oven to 350°.

6. Heat lightly oiled, non-stick skillet over medium heat. Skillet is ready when a drop of water "dances" over the surface.

7. For each dosa, pour ¼ cup batter into skillet. Cook until dosa bottoms are golden brown and firm, 6-8 minutes.

8. Slide cooked dosas onto oiled baking sheet. Continue making dosas with remaining batter. Bake dosas until golden and crisp, about 20 minutes.

Note: Refrigerate leftovers and use within 6 days.

Yield: 3-4 servings

11 Sweets

Coconut Tofu 'Cheesecake'

With tofu replacing cream cheese, this luscious dessert contains no cholesterol or saturated animal fat. The flavor of coconut will melt in your mouth.

8 ounces firm tofu

¼ cup maple syrup or agave nectar
2 tablespoons cashew butter or almond butter
2 teaspoons vanilla extract
½ teaspoon salt

1¼ cups Coconut Milk (page 35)
2 tablespoons agar flakes (or for agar powder see glossary)

2 tablespoons arrowroot mixed in 2 tablespoons water

1 recipe Oat Nut or Chocolate Rice Crust (optional) (page 158)

1. Bring small pot of water to boil. Cut tofu in several pieces, and boil 5 minutes. Rinse tofu under cold water until cool.

2. Place tofu and next 4 ingredients in blender and set aside.

3. Combine milk and agar in pot. Simmer until agar completely dissolves, about 5 minutes, stirring bottom of pot often to keep agar from sticking. Add dissolved arrowroot, stirring continuously until milky mixture thickens, about 30 seconds. Remove from heat.

4. Start blender and slowly pour hot milky mixture through center lid opening of blender. Blend until smooth.

5. Pour mixture into oiled 9" pie plate (or similar-sized dish), with or without prepared crust, as desired, and chill to set.

Note: Refrigerate leftovers and use within 5 days.

Yield: 4-8 servings

Variation: For **Lemon Coconut Tofu 'Cheesecake'**, add to blender in step 2: 2 tablespoons fresh lemon juice, ½ teaspoon lemon extract (or 1-2 teaspoons lemon zest), and 2 tablespoons maple syrup.

Chocolate Tofu 'Cheesecake'

So rich-tasting and chocolatey. So healthy, too!

8 ounces firm tofu

¼ cup sugar (i.e. evaporated cane juice)
¼ cup each: non-dairy chocolate chips and cocoa powder
1 tablespoon peanut butter
2 teaspoons vanilla extract
½ teaspoon salt

1¾ cups non-dairy milk
2 tablespoons agar flakes (or for agar powder see glossary)

2 tablespoons arrowroot mixed in 2 tablespoons water

1 recipe Oat Nut or Chocolate Rice Crust (optional) (page 158)

1. Bring small pot of water to boil. Cut tofu in several pieces, and boil 5 minutes. Rinse tofu under cold water until cool.

2. Place tofu and next 6 ingredients in blender and set aside.

3. Combine milk and agar in pot. Simmer until agar completely dissolves, about 5 minutes, stirring bottom of pot often to keep agar from sticking. Add dissolved arrowroot, stirring continuously until milky mixture thickens, about 30 seconds. Remove from heat.

4. Start blender and slowly pour hot milky mixture through center lid opening of blender. Blend until smooth.

5. Pour mixture into oiled 9" pie plate (or similar-sized dish), with or without prepared crust, as desired, and chill to set.

Note: Refrigerate leftovers and use within 5 days.

Yield: 4-8 servings

Variation: For **Mocha Tofu 'Cheesecake'**, add 1 tablespoon instant coffee (granules or powder) to blender in step 2.

Carob powder is made from ground pods of the carob tree. It has a hint of chocolate flavor, making it an acceptable substitute for cocoa powder. Available raw or roasted, carob is rich in vitamins and minerals—especially calcium, potassium, and natural sugar. When using carob to replace cocoa powder, the amount of sweetener can be cut in half, reflecting the natural sweetness of carob.

Chocolate Tofu 'Mousse'

A rich, velvety smooth dish made incredibly nutritious with tofu.

8 ounces firm tofu

¾ cup non-dairy milk
¼ cup each: cocoa powder and non-dairy chocolate chips
¼ cup sugar (i.e. evaporated cane juice)
1 tablespoon peanut butter or other nut butter
2 teaspoons vanilla extract
¼ teaspoon salt

1. Bring small pot of water to boil. Cut tofu in several pieces, and boil 5 minutes. Rinse tofu under cold water until cool.
2. Place all ingredients in blender and blend until smooth.
3. Chill mousse for firmer texture, if desired.
Note: Refrigerate leftovers and use within 5 days.
Yield: 2-4 servings
Variation: For **Tofu Mocha 'Mousse'**, add 1 tablespoon instant coffee (granules or powder) to blender in step 2.

Chocolate Bean Pudding

With a tantalizing thick texture, this bean-based treat is as nourishing and satisfying as it is chocolatey delicious.

2 cups cooked navy or other beans (page 23)
¾ cup non-dairy milk
¼ cup each: cocoa powder and non-dairy chocolate chips
¼ cup sugar (i.e. evaporated cane juice)
2 tablespoons peanut butter or other nut butter
1 teaspoon vanilla extract
½ teaspoon salt

1. Place all ingredients in blender and blend until smooth, adding a little more milk, if necessary, for smoother consistency.
Note: Pudding will thicken as it chills. If using hot cooked beans, decrease amount of milk to ½ cup, adding more only if smoother consistency is desired.
Refrigerate leftovers and use within 5 days.
Yield: 4 servings
Variation: For **Mocha Bean Pudding**, blend 1 tablespoon instant coffee (granules or powder) with all ingredients.

Millet Pudding

Iron-rich millet blends so creamy and smooth. These wholesome puddings are equally good as treats, snacks, or even breakfasts.

Chocolate Millet Pudding

2 cups cooked millet (page 25)
1 cup non-dairy milk
¼ cup cocoa powder
¼ cup sugar (i.e. evaporated cane juice)
1 tablespoon peanut butter or other nut butter
1 teaspoon vanilla extract
½ teaspoon salt

1. Place all ingredients in blender and blend until smooth, adding a little more milk, if necessary, for smoother consistency.

Note: Pudding will thicken as it chills.

Refrigerate leftovers and use within 5 days.

Yield: 3-4 servings

Variation: For **Mocha Millet Pudding**, blend 1 tablespoon instant coffee (granules or powder) with all ingredients.

For **Chocolate Rice Pudding**, replace cooked millet with cooked brown rice (page 25).

Vanilla Millet Pudding

2 cups cooked millet (page 25)
¾ cup non-dairy milk
¼ cup maple syrup or agave nectar
2 tablespoons cashew butter or almond butter
1 tablespoon vanilla extract
½ teaspoon salt

1. Place all ingredients in blender and blend until smooth, adding a little more milk, if necessary, for smoother consistency.

Note: Pudding will thicken as it chills.

Refrigerate leftovers and use within 5 days.

Yield: 3-4 servings

Variation: For **Vanilla Rice Pudding**, replace cooked millet with cooked brown rice (page 25).

Sweet Potato Pudding

A creamy and flavorful dessert pudding made of sweet potatoes!

3 medium sweet potatoes or yams (peeled, sliced in 1" rounds)

1 cup non-dairy milk
¼ cup dried dates (chopped)
2 tablespoons maple syrup or agave nectar (optional)
1 teaspoon vanilla extract
¼ teaspoon salt

1. In steamer basket, steam potatoes until tender, about 15 minutes.
2. Place potatoes with all ingredients in blender. Blend until smooth.
Note: Refrigerate leftovers and use within 5 days.
Yield: 4-6 servings

Maple Noodle Pudding

An amazing sweet treat that can double as a main dish casserole.

3 cups uncooked whole-grain noodles (about 9 ounces)

1 tablespoon coconut oil or canola oil

8 ounces firm tofu (mashed)

1 recipe Tofu 'Sour Cream' (page 86)
½ cup maple syrup or agave nectar
½ cup pecans or walnuts (chopped)
½ cup raisins or other dried fruit (chopped)
1 medium apple (cored, peeled, and chopped)
2 teaspoons each: cinnamon and vanilla extract
½ teaspoon salt
¼ teaspoon ground turmeric

1. Preheat oven to 350°.
2. Cook noodles in boiling water in pot, until just tender, 8-10 minutes. Drain noodles.
3. Place noodles in bowl. Toss with oil. Add mashed tofu and mix.
4. Stir in remaining ingredients, combining thoroughly.
5. Transfer batter into oiled 8x8" (or similar-sized) glass baking dish.
6. Bake uncovered 40 minutes or until golden. Let cool 10-15 minutes before serving.
Note: Refrigerate leftovers and use within 5 days.
Yield: 4-8 servings

Apple Blueberry Cobbler

There's no bottom crust here. Just lots of juicy fruit with a granola topping.

¾ cup water
¼ cup granulated tapioca (quick-cooking type)
3 tablespoons fresh lemon juice
3 tablespoons maple syrup or agave nectar
1 teaspoon vanilla extract
¼ teaspoon each: cinnamon and salt

3 medium apples (cored, peeled, and chopped)
2 cups blueberries (fresh or frozen)

2 cups Flax-Date Granola (page 43)

1. Preheat oven to 350°.
2. In small bowl, combine first 7 ingredients. Set aside.
3. Combine apples and blueberries in bowl. Stir in tapioca mixture.
4. Transfer mixture to oiled, 8x8" (or similar-sized) glass baking dish. Cover and bake 1 hour.
5. Remove from oven and spread with granola topping.
Note: Refrigerate leftovers and use within 5 days.
Yield: 4-5 servings

Apple Blueberry Tapioca Pudding

A delicate and tangy pudding of apples and blueberries.

3 medium apples (cored, peeled, and chopped)
3 cups blueberries (fresh or frozen)
1 cup water
¾ cup frozen apple juice concentrate (thawed)
2 tablespoons fresh lemon juice
1 teaspoon cinnamon
¼ teaspoon salt

¼ cup small tapioca pearls

1. In pot, combine all ingredients, except tapioca, and bring to boil over medium heat.
2. Slowly whisk tapioca into simmering fruit mixture. Lower heat, cover pot, and simmer 25 minutes, stirring frequently.
3. Chill to firm.
Note: Refrigerate leftovers and use within 5 days.
Yield: 4-6 servings

Fruit Butter

A rich-tasting purée that makes an ideal spread, topping, and sweetener.

1½ cups boiling water
¾ cup each: dried dates and dried apricots (chopped)

2 tablespoons fresh lemon or lime juice
pinch of salt

1. Place water and fruit in bowl. Cover and let stand until cool.
2. Transfer fruit with soak water to blender. Add last 2 ingredients and blend until smooth.

Note: Refrigerate leftovers and use within 7 days.

Yield: about 2¼ cups

Variation: Replace apricots or dates with other dried fruit, such as prunes, figs, mango, or papaya.

Fruity 'Jell-o'

Agar and arrowroot give this flavorful gelatin-free gelled dessert a wondrous custardy texture.

2¾ cups water
1¼ cups frozen apple or berry juice concentrate (thawed)
4 tablespoons agar flakes (or for agar powder see glossary)

2 tablespoons arrowroot mixed in 2 tablespoons water

2 medium apples (cored, peeled, and sliced)
2 medium bananas (sliced)

1. Combine first 3 ingredients in pot. Bring to boil over medium-high heat, stirring bottom of pot often to prevent sticking. Reduce heat and simmer until agar dissolves, about 5 minutes, stirring often. Add dissolved arrowroot, stirring continuously until mixture thickens, about 30 seconds. Remove from heat.
2. Place cut fruit in bowl. Cover with hot mixture. Chill to set.

Note: Refrigerate leftovers and use within 7 days.

Yield: 4-6 servings

Variation: Replace apples and bananas with 4 cups sliced peaches or strawberries.

Apple Bread

A simple, but satisfying cake-like bread.

2 cups homemade oat flour (page 28)
1 cup rolled oats
½ cup sugar (i.e. evaporated cane juice)
2 teaspoons baking powder (aluminum-free)
2 teaspoons cinnamon
½ teaspoon salt

1½ cups apple juice
2 medium apples (cored and chopped)

1 recipe Cinnamon Maple Glaze (page 151)

1. Preheat oven to 350°.
2. In bowl, combine first 6 dry ingredients.
3. In blender, blend juice and apples until smooth.
4. Pour blender mix into bowl of dry ingredients, mixing well.
5. Transfer batter into oiled 8x8" (or similar-sized) glass baking dish.
6. Bake 40 minutes or until golden. Let cool. Spread with glaze.
Note: Refrigerate leftovers and use within 5 days or freeze.
Yield: 6-8 servings
Variation: For **Apple Muffins,** spoon batter into oiled muffin cups and bake 25 minutes, or until golden.

For **Apple Jelly Muffins,** fill each muffin cup about ¾ full of batter. Drop 1 tablespoon strawberry jam or preserves in center of batter in each muffin cup and bake 25 minutes, or until golden.

Ants On A (Snowy) Log

A nutritious snack, with a playful name, that will will delight the senses by combining crunchy, creamy, and chewy textures.

4 celery stalks (rinsed, dried, and ends trimmed)
peanut butter or other nut butter (to taste)
dried, unsweetened, shredded coconut (to taste)
raisins, blueberries, or sunflower seeds (to taste)

1. Cut each celery stalk crosswise in half.
2. Fill hollow groove of each celery piece (log) with nut butter, then sprinkle with coconut (snow), and press in raisins (ants).
Note: Refrigerate leftovers and use within 4 days.
Yield: 2-4 servings
Variation: Replace celery with sliced apple rounds.

Chocolate Brownies

Rich-tasting, fudgy chocolate brownies. Truly a "comfort food."

2 cups homemade oat flour (page 28)
1 cup walnuts or pecans (chopped)
½ cup each: cocoa powder and non-dairy chocolate chips
½ cup sugar (i.e. evaporated cane juice)
¼ cup flax seed meal (page 29)
2 teaspoons baking powder (aluminum-free)
1 teaspoon cinnamon
½ teaspoon salt

2 medium apples (cored and chopped)
1¾ cups non-dairy milk
2 tablespoons peanut butter or other nut butter
1 teaspoon vanilla extract

1-2 recipes Chocolate Sauce (page 152)

1. Preheat oven to 350°.
2. In bowl, combine first 9 dry ingredients.
3. In blender, blend next 4 ingredients until smooth.
4. Pour blender mix into bowl of dry ingredients, mixing well.
5. Transfer batter into oiled 8x8" (or similar-sized) glass baking dish.
6. Bake 40 minutes. Let cool. Spread with sauce, and cut in squares.
Note: Refrigerate leftovers and use within 5 days or freeze.
Yield: 6-8 servings

Chocolate for centuries has been seen both as a remedy for a broken heart, and for creating a feeling that mimics that of being in love. As it turns out, there's an edgy side, too. Chocolate contains natural compounds that resemble the chemical structures in marijuana. Natural cannabinoids, as well as caffeine, and phenylethylamine—all found in chocolate—are why most people find this "food of the gods" so appealing and addictive.

Chocolate (Broccoli) Cake

Packed with broccoli, this dark chocolate cake is incredibly moist and fudgy.
Let everyone know when the cake's ready—but don't mention "broccoli."

4 cups raw broccoli florets (cut in bite-sized pieces)

2 cups homemade oat flour (page 28)
½ cup each: non-dairy chocolate chips and cocoa powder
½ cup sugar (i.e. evaporated cane juice)
¼ cup flax seed meal (page 29)
2 teaspoons baking powder (aluminum-free)
2 teaspoons cinnamon
½ teaspoon salt

2 cups non-dairy milk
2 tablespoons peanut butter or other nut butter
2 teaspoons vanilla extract

1-2 recipes Chocolate Sauce (page 152)

1. Preheat oven to 350°.
2. Place broccoli in steamer basket and steam 3 minutes.
3. In bowl, combine next 8 dry ingredients.
4. In blender, blend broccoli, milk, peanut butter, and vanilla, until smooth.
5. Pour blender mix into bowl of dry ingredients, mixing well.
6. Transfer batter into oiled 8x8" (or similar-sized) glass baking dish.
7. Bake 40 minutes. Let cool. Spread with sauce.

Note: Refrigerate leftovers and use within 5 days or freeze.
Yield: 6-8 servings
Variation: For **Mocha (Broccoli) Cake**, add 1-2 tablespoons instant coffee (granules or powder) to blender ingredients.

Broccoli has more absorbable calcium than does dairy milk. Along with family members kale, collards, and bok choy, broccoli is among the elite vegetable cancer-fighters. These four plants are especially rich in various phytochemicals that block cancer-causing substances from reaching cells, that neutralize free radicals, and that inhibit the spread of cancerous cells.

Millet Cornbread

This sweet version of an all-American quickbread replaces cornmeal with freshly-made millet flour. It's moist, crumbly, and a delight to eat.

2 cups homemade millet flour (page 28)
½ cup flax seed meal (page 29)
2 teaspoons baking powder (aluminum-free)
½ teaspoon salt

1¼ cups non-dairy milk
½ cup raw almonds or other nuts

½ cup maple syrup or agave nectar
1 cup corn kernels (fresh or frozen and thawed)
1 medium apple (cored and chopped)
1 teaspoon vanilla extract

1 recipe Cinnamon Maple Glaze (page 151)

1. Preheat oven to 350°.
2. In bowl, combine first 4 dry ingredients.
3. In blender, blend milk and almonds until smooth.
4. Add next 4 ingredients to blender and blend until smooth.
5. Pour blender mix into bowl of dry ingredients, mixing well.
6. Transfer batter into oiled 8x8" (or similar-sized) glass baking dish.
7. Bake 40 minutes or until golden. Let cool. Spread with glaze.

Note: Refrigerate leftovers and use within 5 days or freeze.

Yield: 6-8 servings

Variation: For **Millet Corn Muffins,** spoon batter into oiled muffin cups and bake 25 minutes, or until golden.

Orange Bean Cake

A heavenly orange scent and flavor permeate this moist, dense cake.

2 cups homemade oat flour (page 28)
2 teaspoons baking powder (aluminum-free)
½ teaspoon salt

2 cups cooked navy or other white beans (page 23)
½ cup each: water and frozen orange juice concentrate
½ cup maple syrup or agave nectar
1 teaspoon orange extract

1 recipe Orange Maple Glaze (page 151)

1. Preheat oven to 350°.
2. In bowl, combine first 3 dry ingredients.
3. In blender, blend next 5 ingredients until smooth.
4. Pour blender mix into bowl of dry ingredients, mixing well.
5. Transfer batter into oiled 8x8" (or similar-sized) glass baking dish.
6. Bake 40 minutes or until golden. Let cool. Spread with glaze.
Note: Refrigerate leftovers and use within 5 days or freeze.
Yield: 6-8 servings
Variation: For **Orange Bean Muffins,** spoon batter into oiled muffin cups and bake 25 minutes, or until golden.

Oranges of any type that are ripe and full of juice will be firm and heavy for their size. Navel oranges are seedless, thick-skinned eating oranges with an often-amusing belly-button. Valencia oranges, preferred for juicing, have thin, smooth skin, and numerous seeds. All oranges are tree-ripened and usually look green when harvested. If subjected to cold temperatures (or gassed or dyed) these fully ripe, green oranges turn orange. So, an orange with a greenish tint makes excellent eating and is usually very sweet. Before cutting into an orange, scrub it with soap and hot water to remove any dirt or bacteria on its skin that could be transferred to the fruit's flesh.

Sweet Potato Muffins

Tender, sweet, russet-colored muffins studded with morsels of dried apricot.

3 medium sweet potatoes or yams (peeled, sliced in 1" rounds)

2 cups homemade oat flour (page 28)
¼ cup flax seed meal (page 29)
2 teaspoons each: cinnamon and baking powder (alum.-free)
½ teaspoon salt

1¾ cups non-dairy milk
½ cup maple syrup or agave nectar
2 teaspoons vanilla extract
1 cup dried apricots (chopped) or other dried fruit

1. Preheat oven to 350°.
2. In steamer basket, steam potatoes 15 minutes. Set aside.
3. In bowl, combine oat flour and next 4 dry ingredients.
4. In separate bowl, mash potatoes and combine with last 4 ingredients. Pour into bowl of dry ingredients, mixing well.
5. Fill oiled muffin cups and bake 25 minutes, or until golden.
Note: Refrigerate leftovers and use within 5 days or freeze.
Yield: 12 muffins

Lemon Tofu 'Pound Cake'

Pure bliss when spread with Cinnamon Maple Glaze (page 151).

2 cups homemade oat flour (page 28)
2 teaspoons each: lemon zest and baking powder (alum.-free)
¼ teaspoon salt

16 ounces firm tofu
¾ cup maple syrup or agave nectar
¼ cup each: fresh lemon juice and non-dairy milk
1 teaspoon each: lemon extract and vanilla extract

1. Preheat oven to 350°.
2. In bowl, combine first 4 dry ingredients.
3. In blender, blend next 6 wet ingredients until smooth.
4. Pour blender mix into bowl of dry ingredients, mixing well.
5. Transfer batter into oiled 8x8" (or similar-sized) glass baking dish.
6. Bake 45 minutes or until golden.
Note: Refrigerate leftovers and use within 5-7 days.
Yield: 4-5 servings

Sweet Crescent Rolls

Tender, rich-tasting sweet rolls filled with chocolate and coconut.

½ cup oat flour (see note)
¼ cup each: brown rice flour and garbanzo bean flour
¼ cup sugar (i.e. evaporated cane juice)
3 tablespoons flax seed meal (page 29)
1 teaspoon baking powder (aluminum-free)
1 teaspoon cinnamon
¼ teaspoon salt

¾ cup non-dairy milk
1½ tablespoons cashew or almond butter
1 teaspoon vanilla extract

½ cup non-dairy chocolate chips
¼ cup dried, unsweetened shredded coconut

1. Preheat oven to 350°.
2. Place first 8 dry ingredients in bowl.
3. In small bowl, whisk next 3 wet ingredients.
4. Transfer wet ingredients to bowl of dry ingredients, mixing to form a stiff dough. Let dough rest 5 minutes.
5. Place dough on floured surface. Briefly knead, adding more oat flour, to form firm dough ball. Let dough rest 5 minutes.
6. Roll dough to 10" diameter circle. Cut into 8 wedges (like a pie).
7. On each wedge, spread about 1 tablespoon chocolate chips and about 1½ teaspoons coconut, pressing down to embed ingredients in dough. Roll each wedge, from base to tip. Curve ends to make crescent shapes.
8. Place rolls on oiled baking sheet. Bake 30 minutes or until golden.
Note: I recommend store-bought oat flour (instead of homemade) for finer pastry texture.
Refrigerate leftovers and use within 5 days or freeze.
Yield: 4 servings (8 rolls)
Variation: Replace chocolate chips and coconut with 1 tablespoon berry jam or other fruit preserves on each wedge.

Cinnamon Sticky Buns

Sweet, gooey, hearty sticky buns that'll make you think you're dreaming. Enjoy them piping hot as a treat, snack, or breakfast.

½ recipe Basic Dough (page 29)

3 tablespoons sugar (i.e. evaporated cane juice)
3 tablespoons non-dairy milk
3 tablespoons flax seed meal (page 29)
2 tablespoons peanut butter or other nut butter
1 teaspoon each: cinnamon and vanilla extract
¼ teaspoon salt

½ cup pecans or walnuts (finely chopped)
3 tablespoons each: non-dairy chocolate chips (optional)
and dried, unsweetened shredded coconut (optional)

1 recipe Cinnamon Maple Glaze (page 151)

1. Preheat oven to 400°.
2. On floured surface, roll dough to about 8x12" rectangle.
3. Combine next 7 ingredients and spread evenly over dough.
4. Combine nuts, chocolate chips, and coconut and sprinkle over dough, pressing down to embed ingredients in dough.
5. Roll up dough on large side to form a firm log. Slice log into 10-12 equal pieces and place cut-side down, close together in oiled 8x8" (or similar-sized) glass baking dish.
6. Bake 25 minutes or until golden. Drizzle buns with glaze.
Note: Refrigerate leftovers and use within 5 days.
Yield: 3-6 servings
Variation: Replace glaze with Cashew Sauce (to taste) (page 151).

Blueberry 'Yogurt'

A delicious, creamy, maple-sweetened berry "yogurt" without any artificial flavorings, stabilizers, or gelatin.

1 recipe Tofu 'Sour Cream' (page 86)
1 cup blueberries (fresh or frozen and thawed)
3 tablespoons maple syrup or agave nectar
1 teaspoon vanilla extract

1. Blend all ingredients until smooth.
Note: Refrigerate leftovers and use within 5 days.
Yield: 2-3 servings

Maple Glazes

Topping any hot or cold dish with these maple-sweetened glazes will elicit instant delight.

Cinnamon Maple Glaze

3 tablespoons maple syrup or agave nectar
1 tablespoon coconut oil or non-dairy margarine
½ teaspoon each: cinnamon and vanilla extract
pinch of salt

1. Place all ingredients in pot and briefly warm over low heat, stirring until thoroughly combined.

Note: Refrigerate leftovers and use within 10 days.

Yield: about ¼ cup

Orange Maple Glaze

2 tablespoons maple syrup or agave nectar
2 tablespoons frozen orange juice concentrate
1 tablespoon coconut oil or non-dairy margarine

1. Place all ingredients in pot and briefly warm over low heat, stirring until thoroughly combined.

Note: Refrigerate leftovers and use within 7 days.

Yield: about ¼ cup

Cashew Sauce & Frosting

Seductively luscious, yet nutritious, this incredible topping will grace cookies, pies, cereals, or fruit—you name it!

½ cup cashew butter
¼ cup coconut oil
¼ cup maple syrup or agave nectar
1 teaspoon vanilla extract
½ teaspoon fresh lemon juice
¼ teaspoon salt

1. Place all ingredients in pot. Briefly heat over low heat, stirring until thoroughly combined.

Note: As a sauce, serve it warm or at room temperature. For a thick frosting, chill in refrigerator until it sets, at least 4-6 hours.

Refrigerate leftovers and use within 7 days.

Yield: about 1 cup

Chocolate Sauce

Without a speck of dairy-milk, butter, or white sugar, this ambrosial sauce will win over even hard-core chocolate lovers. Break out the spoons!

½ cup cocoa powder
½ cup sugar (i.e. evaporated cane juice)
¼ teaspoon each: salt and cinnamon

½ cup non-dairy milk

1 tablespoon peanut butter or other nut butter
1 tablespoon coconut oil (melted) or non-dairy margarine
1 teaspoon vanilla extract

1. In bowl, combine first 4 dry ingredients.
2. Add milk and mix thoroughly.
3. Stir in remaining ingredients, adding more milk as necessary, for smooth consistency.
Note: Refrigerate leftovers and use within 7 days.
Yield: about 1 cup

Chocolate Date Sauce

Rich, smooth, fruit-sweetened—and oh, so chocolatey!

2¼ cups non-dairy milk
1½ cups dried dates (chopped)

¾ cup cocoa powder
2 tablespoons peanut butter or other nut butter
2 teaspoons vanilla extract
½ teaspoon salt

1. Combine milk and dates in bowl. Cover and refrigerate at least 2 hours for dates to soften.
2. Transfer milk, dates, and remaining ingredients to blender and blend until smooth.
Note: Refrigerate leftovers and use within 7 days.
Yield: about 3 cups

Tofu 'Whipped Cream'

No need for whipped cream loaded with saturated fat, sugar, stabilizers, and emulsifiers. Instead, try this wholesome cream topping on all the usual places.

8 ounces firm tofu

½ cup maple syrup or agave nectar
2 tablespoons cashew butter
2 teaspoons vanilla extract
½ teaspoon salt

1¼ cups Coconut Milk (page 35) or other non-dairy milk
2 tablespoons agar flakes (or for agar powder see glossary)

2 tablespoons arrowroot mixed in 2 tablespoons water

1. Bring pot of water to boil. Cut tofu in several pieces, and boil 5 minutes. Rinse tofu under cold water until cool.

2. Place tofu and next 4 ingredients in blender. Set aside.

3. Combine milk and agar in pot. Simmer until agar dissolves, about 5 minutes, stirring often to keep agar from sticking. Add dissolved arrowroot, stirring continuously until milky mixture thickens, about 30 seconds. Remove from heat.

4. Start blender and slowly pour hot milky mixture through center lid opening of blender. Blend until smooth.

5. Transfer mixture to bowl. Chill to set. Then whisk until smooth.

Note: Refrigerate leftovers and use within 7 days.

Yield: about 2½ cups

Naturally-colored frosting or whipped cream will bring joy when you present your cakes or treats. For best results, mix in your coloring within a few hours of planning to use your topping. Add your coloring a little at a time until you reach the desired hue. For yellow, add a pinch of ground turmeric. For green, try liquid chlorophyll (available at health food stores). Purple results from the addition of blueberry juice. Red or pink emerges when a little red juice is whisked in (sources include beet, cherry, and cranberry juices).

Chocolate 'Truffles'

Addictive little chocolate candies with rich, nutty centers.

¼ cup dried, unsweetened shredded coconut

¼ cup maple syrup or agave nectar
2 tablespoons coconut oil
2 tablespoons peanut butter or other nut butter
1 teaspoon vanilla extract

½ cup pecans, walnuts, or cashews (chopped)
½ cup dried, unsweetened shredded coconut
½ cup raisins or other dried fruit (chopped)
¼ cup each: cocoa powder and non-dairy chocolate chips
¼ teaspoon salt

1. Place ¼ cup shredded coconut in bowl and set aside.

2. Place next 4 ingredients in pot and heat briefly on low heat, mixing well. Add next 6 ingredients, mixing well. Remove from heat.

3. When mixture is cool to the touch, use moistened hands to pinch off small pieces to form 16-18 balls. Roll each in reserved coconut in bowl. Place balls on plate. Chill or freeze to harden.

Note: Keep refrigerated. Use within 7 days or freeze.

Yield: 16-18 truffles

Chocolate Brittle

Hearty chunks of chocolate—truly a sublime melt-in-your-mouth experience.

¾ cup coconut oil
½ cup each: cocoa powder and sugar (i.e. evap. cane juice)
2 tablespoons peanut butter or other nut butter
1 teaspoon vanilla extract
¼ teaspoon salt

¾ cup dried apricots (chopped)
½ cup roasted nuts (chopped) (page 30)

1. Place all ingredients, except apricots and nuts, in pot and heat briefly over low heat, mixing well. Stir in apricots and nuts.

2. Spread mixture in glass dish. Let cool 5 minutes, then cover and freeze 1 hour to harden. Remove and cut or break into chunks.

Note: Keep in refrigerator or freezer and use within 14 days.

Variation: Stir ½ cup dried, unsweetened shredded coconut with apricots and nuts.

Chocolate Chip 'Macaroons'

A chocolate and coconut lover's dream come true. A bit crisp outside, and melt-in-your-mouth gooey inside. There is no having just one!

1 cup dried, unsweetened shredded coconut
1 cup Coconut Flour (see below)
½ cup non-dairy chocolate chips
¼ cup flax seed meal (page 29)
½ teaspoon salt

¼ cup maple syrup or agave nectar
¼ cup non-dairy milk
1 teaspoon vanilla extract

1. Preheat oven to 325°.
2. In bowl, combine first 5 dry ingredients.
3. In separate bowl, combine next 3 wet ingredients.
4. Pour wet ingredients into bowl of dry ingredients and mix thoroughly. Let dough rest 5 minutes.
5. With wet hands, form dough into small balls.
6. Place balls on oiled baking sheet and flatten into 2" rounds.
7. Bake 25 minutes. Remove from oven and flip macaroons. Bake 15 minutes more or until golden.

Note: Refrigerate leftovers and use within 5 days or freeze.
Yield: about 16 macaroons

Coconut Flour

A delicate, sweet flour easily made with a blender. Use it to add a light coconutty touch to quickbreads. And, to make some macaroons.

3¾ cups dried, unsweetened shredded coconut

1. Place 1¼ cups coconut in blender and grind into flour, about 60 seconds, stopping blender to shake and stir flour, as necessary.
2. Continue with remaining coconut as above.

Note: Use coconut flour to replace up to ¼ of the "regular" flour in any quickbread recipe.

Refrigerate leftover flour and use within 14 days or freeze.
Yield: about 3 cups

Chocolate Chip Cookies

A comforting classic if ever there were one. Yet these delicious chocolatey cookies are made with beans and whole-grains!

1 cup each: brown rice flour and garbanzo bean flour
½ cup non-dairy chocolate chips
¼ cup sugar (i.e. evaporated cane juice)
¼ cup flax seed meal (page 29)
2 teaspoons baking powder (aluminum-free)
1 teaspoon cinnamon
½ teaspoon salt

1 cup non-dairy milk
3 tablespoons peanut butter or other nut butter
1 teaspoon vanilla extract

1. Preheat oven to 350°.
2. In bowl, combine first 8 dry ingredients in bowl.
3. In blender, blend next 3 wet ingredients until smooth.
4. Pour blender mix into bowl of dry ingredients, mixing well.
5. With wet hands, form dough into small balls.
6. Place balls on oiled baking sheet and gently flatten.
7. Bake 20 minutes or until lightly browned.
Note: Refrigerate leftovers and use within 5 days or freeze.
Yield: about 16 cookies
Variation: For **Thumbprint Cookies**, place dough balls on oiled baking sheet. Make crater at center of each and fill with jelly.

Peanuts are susceptible to a toxic mold called aflatoxin. Studies have shown that the major brands of peanut butter are generally safe, but that significant levels of aflatoxin are likely present in freshly-made peanut butter ground in retail stores. Peanuts grown and stored in humid areas (i.e. Southeastern U.S.) are more likely to harbor aflatoxin than are peanuts from such arid, Southwestern states as New Mexico.

Oatmeal Raisin Cookies

Few treats are more satisfying than these moist, chewy classics.

1½ cups rolled oats
1 cup homemade oat flour (page 28)
¾ cup raisins
¼ cup sugar (i.e. evaporated cane juice)
2 teaspoons baking powder (aluminum-free)
2 teaspoons cinnamon
½ teaspoon salt

1 cup apple juice or non-dairy milk

1. Preheat oven to 350°.
2. In bowl, combine first 7 dry ingredients.
3. Pour liquid into bowl of dry ingredients and mix well.
4. With wet hands, form dough into small balls.
5. Place balls on oiled baking sheet and flatten into 3" rounds.
6. Bake 15 minutes or until lightly browned.
Note: Refrigerate leftovers and use within 5 days or freeze.
Yield: about 12 cookies

Oat Brittle

This oat based "peanut brittle" delivers plenty of sweetness and crunch.

2½ cups rolled oats
½ cup pecans, cashews, or walnuts (chopped)
½ cup non-dairy chocolate chips
½ teaspoon each: cinnamon and salt

½ cup brown rice syrup
2 tablespoons peanut butter or other nut butter
2 tablespoons coconut oil
1 teaspoon vanilla extract

1. Preheat oven to 225°.
2. Combine first 5 dry ingredients in bowl.
3. Briefly heat next 4 ingredients in pot, stirring until smooth. Add to bowl of dry ingredients and thoroughly combine.
4. Spread mixture on oiled baking sheet and bake 45 minutes.
5. Remove from oven. Let cool, then crack in small pieces.
Note: Refrigerate leftovers and use within 7 days.
Yield: 6-8 servings

Oat Nut Crust

A cookie-like crust for any pie or no-bake "cheesecake" filling.

1½ cups rolled oats
½ cup pecans, cashews, or walnuts
¼ teaspoon each: cinnamon and salt

¼ cup maple syrup or agave nectar
2 tablespoons coconut oil
2 teaspoons vanilla extract

1. Preheat oven to 350°.
2. Blend first 4 ingredients in blender into a meal. Transfer to bowl.
3. Combine remaining ingredients in pot and briefly warm over low heat and stir until combined. Add to bowl of oat and nut meal and mix well.
4. Press mixture into bottom and sides of oiled 9" pie plate.
5. Bake until lightly browned, about 10 minutes. Cool before filling.
Yield: one 9" pie crust

Chocolate Rice Crust

A delicate, nourishing crumbly crust that's great for any pie or no-bake "cheesecake" filling.

¾ cup brown rice flour
2 tablespoons cocoa powder
½ teaspoon baking powder (aluminum-free)
¼ teaspoon each: cinnamon and salt

¼ cup maple syrup or agave nectar
¼ cup non-dairy chocolate chips
2 tablespoons each: peanut butter and coconut oil
2 teaspoons vanilla extract

1. Preheat oven to 350°.
2. Combine first 5 dry ingredients in bowl.
3. Combine remaining wet ingredients in pot and briefly warm over low heat and stir until combined.
4. Pour wet mixture into bowl of dry ingredients and mix well.
5. Press mixture into bottom and sides of oiled 9" pie plate.
6. Bake until lightly browned, about 10 minutes. Cool before filling.
Yield: one 9" pie crust

12 Glossary

CAROB POWDER

SHOYU

GLUTEN

NUTRITIONAL YEAST

TEMPEH

MISO

TAHINI

Agar

Agar (also called agar-agar) is a natural, vegetarian gelatin made from a sea vegetable. It's widely available in flakes and powder. While agar flakes sold in health food stores can be a bit pricey, agar powder sold in Asian markets is more reasonably priced. Flakes and powder are interchangeable, though not in equal measures.

Agar powder is about 5 times as effective a gelling agent as agar flakes. So 1 tablespoon powder can be substituted for 5 tablespoons flakes. Since the various brands of agar powder may differ in gelling strength, it is necessary to experiment with them to determine what quantities are needed to gel particular dishes. Some people notice a slight "fishy" or sea-taste when using the powder, especially in desserts. The flakes would be appropriate since there are no off-tastes to them. Agar lasts indefinitely when stored in an airtight container in a cool, dry spot.

Agave Nectar (see Sweeteners)

Amaranth (see Grains)

Arrowroot

This natural starch is derived from the whole root of a tropical plant and replaces overly-processed cornstarch, measure for measure, as a thickener. It thickens at a lower temperature than does cornstarch and is free of any chalky taste. Since arrowroot sold in small jars can be expensive, look for it in bulk containers at health food stores.

Artificial Sweeteners (see Sweeteners)

Baking Powder

When purchasing baking powder, avoid brands that contain aluminum compounds (check label) as aluminum is toxic and possibly linked to Alzheimer's Disease. With time, baking powder goes "flat." When you open a can, write the date on the lid. Check after 6 months by stirring 1 teaspoon baking powder into ½ cup hot water. The reaction should be immediate foaming and fizzing. If not, toss the powder.

Beans

While there are hundreds of varieties of beans, my focus in this book has been on a few widely-available ones: pinto beans, navy beans, garbanzo beans, kidney beans, black beans, lima beans, soybeans, split peas, and lentils.

Although packaged dried beans are readily available in supermarkets and groceries, I prefer to buy dried beans in health food stores from the bulk bins. Since health food stores move lots of beans quickly in and out of their stores, the beans are fresher, tastier, and more nutritious than their bagged counterparts.

Store dried beans in airtight containers in a cool spot away from sunlight. They'll last up to a year, although it's best to use them within 3 months of purchase. While canned beans are not as fresh, nutritious, or economical as home-cooked dried beans, they can be handy at times. Drain and rinse canned beans before use.

A few words about gas. Beans contain complex sugars that can pass into the colon undigested where local bacteria have a field day feasting on these sugars, creating gas. However, there are a few things that can be done to reduce the problem:

• Soaking beans and discarding the soaking water is an effective way to get rid of a lot of the hard-to-digest sugars. One method is to soak the beans overnight (or 6-8 hours) in 4 times their volume of cold water (in the refrigerator to keep the beans from fermenting during the soak). Then discard the soaking water and cook the beans in fresh water. The other method is the "quick-soak." Place the beans in a pot with 4 times their volume of cold water, bring to a boil, and then remove from the heat for 1-2 hours. Discard the soaking water, replace with fresh water, and cook. *Note:* Split peas, adzuki beans, and lentils do not need to be soaked prior to cooking.

• Consume modest quantities of beans at first—¼ to ½ cup cooked beans at a time—and start off doing this just a few times per week until your system adjusts to beans. In time, you can eat beans more often and increase the amount to fill your needs.

• Make sure the beans have been thoroughly cooked (soft when you squeeze them) since they'll digest better. Some people purchase liquid enzymes available in health food stores to aid in the digestion of beans.

Note: Before dried beans are to be soaked, they need to be sorted through to remove any stones or other foreign matter. Give them a thorough rinsing before soaking.

Blackstrap Molasses (see Sweeteners)

Brewer's Yeast (see Nutritional Yeast)

Brown Rice (see Grains, and Flours)

Brown Rice Syrup (see Sweeteners)

Buckwheat (see Grains)

Canola Oil (see Oils)

Capers

Capers are small, unopened flower buds from the caper bush, a small shrub that grows all around the Mediterranean Sea. They're usually available in small jars packed in a vinegar brine. These small tart nuggets will offer a pleasantly sharp, almost lemony flavor to salads, sauces, condiments, and even pizza toppings. 1-2 tablespoons in a recipe will do nicely.

Capers should be rinsed before using and will keep for months in the refrigerator as long as they remain covered by the brine.

Carob Powder

Made from the dried pods of a Mediterranean tree, carob powder looks and tastes a little like cocoa powder and is naturally rich in fiber and calcium. Available raw or roasted (equally tasty), carob powder should be stored in an airtight container in a cool, dry spot. Use it in place of cocoa powder measure-for-measure in any recipe.

Coconut Oil (see Oils)

Cornmeal (see Flours)

Edamame (see Soyfoods)

Evaporated Cane Juice (see Sweeteners)

Fake Meats

Health food stores sell meatless hot dogs, burgers, chicken nuggets, bacon, cold cuts, and many other meat look-and-taste-alikes. They are made primarily from an unwholesome ingredient called "soy protein isolate."

Similar to "hydrolyzed protein," "textured vegetable protein" (T.V.P.), or just plain "soy protein," these isolates are made from soybeans or other plant proteins using extreme processing methods including solvent baths, acid rinses, high heat, and pressure.

The result is as unnatural a product as can be. Since ours is the first generation to consume products made with such altered soy protein, the long term health risks are not yet known. Common sense would dictate avoiding such products. If eaten at all, they should be eaten infrequently and in small quantities.

Fake meats often are made using seitan (also known as "wheat meat") which is made of wheat gluten. Gluten has been described here in the glossary as an unwholesome food fraught with danger for tens of millions of Americans. As with the protein isolates, seitan should be eaten infrequently, if at all, and certainly not by those with sensitivities to gluten.

Flax Seed Meal

It would be hard to imagine a more potent, health-promoting food than flax seeds. A little bigger than sesame seeds, flax seeds have hard, shiny shells reflecting their golden or brown colors. In order to reap the incredible benefits of flax seeds, you must first grind them into a meal (or powder) using a blender or small coffee or spice grinder.

Flax seeds are notable as a potent source of omega-3 essential fatty acids. These fatty acids are believed to provide protection against a wide array of conditions, including heart disease, rheumatoid arthritis, skin disorders, and other inflammatory and autoimmune conditions.

Flax seeds are an extremely rich source of lignans, estrogen-like, fibrous compounds proven to be powerful anti-cancer agents. While lignans are found in grains, fruits, and vegetables, they are by far most abundant of all in flax seeds.

Lignans protect against breast and prostate cancer by landing on hormone-sensitive body sites (receptors) and blocking the arrival of human estrogen and testosterone—potent cancer-stimulating hormones. In this manner, lignans protect sensitive tissues in much the same way as do the powerful isoflavones (plant chemicals) found in soy products.

Research confirms that lignans are capable of slowing and stopping breast and prostate tumor cells from multiplying out of control. In a 2007 study from Duke University, prostate-cancer patients who added 3 tablespoons of flax seed meal to their daily diets exhibited remarkable results. Their cancer cells were found to be dividing at a much slower rate than expected and there was an increased death of tumor cells. Their cancer cells were shrinking.

In a University of Toronto study (published in 2005) of women recently diagnosed with breast cancer, the addition of 2 tablespoons of flax seed meal each day resulted in a significant slowing of their rate of cancer cell growth.

Lignans are also believed responsible for reducing the amount of "bad" artery-clogging cholesterol and for exerting a leveling effect on blood sugar—especially valuable for diabetics. And, the fiber found in flax seed meal builds stool bulk, promoting intestinal contractions which move waste more quickly out of the body.

Nutritionists recommend 2-3 tablespoons of flax seed meal each day as the therapeutic dose. They advise those who are new to flax seed meal to introduce it gradually, starting with 1-2 teaspoons each day and increasing water intake as well to cover this increase in fiber.

Flax seed meal can be blended with smoothies and stirred into fruit juice, apple sauce, and yogurt. It can be added to hot or cold cereals and even incorporated into casseroles and quickbreads. Store the whole seeds in the refrigerator, and keep the ground flax seed meal in an airtight container in the freezer for up to 3 months.

Flax Seed Oil (see Oils)

Flours (whole and gluten-free)

Those wishing to explore the world of flours beyond wheat flour will find a variety of widely available gluten-free flours made of corn, garbanzo beans, millet, oats, and brown rice. Other distinctive gluten-free flours are made from buckwheat, amaranth, and quinoa. These can replace all or part of the "regular" flour to create nourishing quickbreads with textures and flavors not realized with the traditional use of refined wheat flour.

These flours are usually available at health food stores in either bulk bins or pre-packaged bags. Check the "use-by" dates if purchasing packaged flour and look for at least 6 months left to go before it expires. Store all purchased flours in airtight containers in the refrigerator or freezer for up to six months.

• **Brown Rice Flour**—is a fine, powdery flour with a distinct and earthy brown rice flavor. As with other gluten-free flours, it produces a delicate crumb texture in quickbreads.

• **Cornmeal**—available in several different textures. Look for either "stone-ground" or "unrefined" (as well as "organic"). For making cornbread, muffins, or pancakes, choose either a fine or medium-ground cornmeal.

• **Garbanzo Bean Flour** (chickpea flour)—a high-protein flour made from dried (unroasted) garbanzo beans that gives baked goods and pancakes a sweet, rich, nutty flavor. It is more digestible than the other legume flours.

• **Millet Flour**—can be store-bought or homemade with a blender (page 28). Millet flour imparts a mildly sweet flavor and lends a pale golden hue and crumbly texture to quickbreads.

• **Oat Flour**—lends a sweet, oaty, and delicate crumb to quickbreads. Quick and easy to make homemade oat flour with a blender (page 28) which can be used interchangeably with store-bought oat flour.

Fructose (see Sweeteners)

Garbanzo Bean Flour (see Flours)

Gluten

Americans are crazy about wheat. Every day, every meal is likely to see wheat on the table. Toast, cereal, or pancakes for breakfast are followed by a noontime sandwich, then wrapped up with a big pasta dish or pizza. And, maybe cookies, cakes, and pies tossed in somewhere. All made of wheat. All packed with gluten.

Gluten is the "gluey" protein which provides cohesiveness and structure to products made with wheat and related grains.

Common Grains Containing Gluten

• wheat	• triticale
• barley	• kamut
• rye	• spelt

Common Gluten-Free Grains

• rice	• oats
• millet	• buckwheat
• quinoa	• corn
• wild rice	• amaranth
• sorghum	• teff

While oats by nature do not contain gluten, there is the potential for oats to be contaminated with trace amounts of gluten during processing. Gluten-free oats are available (usually at twice the regular price) indicating that the oats were not processed in facilities containing gluten products.

Why all this attention on gluten? Because gluten plays a major role in many diseases. About 1% of the U.S. population suffers from "celiac disease," a serious autoimmune disorder of the intestinal tract, caused by consuming gluten. Mild symptoms include gas, bloating, and loose stools. Severe ones include weight loss, malabsorption, and malnutrition—serious life-threatening conditions.

In addition, it is estimated that nearly 100 million Americans are intolerant of gluten. This "sensitivity" is a non-celiac condition manifesting in a wide range of troublesome reactions. These include bellyaches, headaches, skin rashes, joint aches, constant fatigue, sinus ailments—to name just a few.

A gluten-free diet is the surest way to test if these symptoms are caused by gluten. Such a diet that eliminates gluten often can be helpful for those with gastrointestinal diseases, such as Crohn's Disease, Ulcerative Colitis, Esophageal Reflex, and Irritable Bowl Syndrome, since gluten is often the trigger for such autoimmune diseases. In addition to those gluten-containing grains, gluten is a common ingredient in many commercially-prepared products.

On the other hand, the majority of Americans seems able to "handle" gluten without exhibiting outward symptoms. But, it's very likely that the continued excess consumption of gluten products could result in chronic damage of the intestines, causing a spate of diseases down the road for this "healthy" population.

The problem with gluten goes way back. Although humans have inhabited the planet for some 2 million years, grains have only been cultivated for the last 10-15,000 years. Which means for nearly all of our existence on earth, we humans have never consumed grains. Maybe the problem is because we haven't had the time to adjust to this "new" discovery in our period on earth. To make matters worse, of all the grains, the gluten-containing grains have the most difficult molecular structure to digest. And the genetic modifications that wheat has undergone have given this most-consumed grain an even greater gluten content.

It's important to be wary of commercially-prepared gluten-free breads. While they contain no gluten, they also contain very little nutrition. Their ingredients mostly include refined (white) rice flour and starches. The most nourishing option is to bake your own homemade breads using the recipes included in this book as the starting point.

For those able to "handle" gluten, whole wheat breads and sprouted whole wheat breads offer more nutrition than refined wheat breads. But, consuming as little wheat products as possible would benefit all. There is no nutritional requirement for gluten.

Those who have only mild sensitivity to gluten may find themselves able to tolerate sprouted whole wheat breads since the sprouting process breaks down the gluten into more digestible chunks. They should read the ingredients label and make sure only sprouted grains are used, and that no gluten is added.

Grains (whole and gluten-free)

Whole grains are grains that still have the bran and germ layers attached to the endosperm (starch) layer. Steer clear of refined grains and their products (such as white rice and white bread). They've had all the nutritious germ and bran stripped away in order to prolong the shelf life of the grains and their products.

Cooked grains can be kept in a covered container in the refrigerator for almost a week or for longer periods in the freezer. Purchase whole grains from the bulk bins of health food stores. These stores have a faster turnover than supermarkets, ensuring fresher grains. Avoid any grains sold in bags, since they could be quite old and dry, resulting in a poor quality product when cooked.

Store grains in airtight containers in the refrigerator or freezer. Although most grains can be kept for many months if properly stored, it's better to purchase small quantities and use them up fairly quickly.

The following whole grains are used in this book:

• **Amaranth** seeds are as tiny as poppy seeds, and pack a considerable amount of calcium and protein. Cooked alone, amaranth can be gummy, but when cooked with another grain, it yields a delicate, nutty flavor with an agreeable texture (page 25).

• **Brown Rice** is a term that can be used to designate any whole grain rice.

  - **brown basmati rice** has long, slender grains (much like long-grain brown rice) and when being cooked will fill your kitchen with a delightful fragrance. It has a unique nutty flavor and chewy texture, and can be used in any recipe for long-grain brown rice.

  - **long-grain brown rice** has long, slender kernels which cook to a dry, fluffy texture. As the grains remain separate after cooking, long-grain is well suited for use in bean dishes, salads, and as a bed of grains for stir-fried vegetables. It's the most commonly-eaten type of brown rice.

  - **short-grain brown rice** kernels are small and plump. When cooked they become soft, tender, slightly sweet, and a bit chewy. Short-grain is somewhat sticky, making it ideal in casseroles, rice puddings, baked goods, croquettes, and sushi.

• **Buckwheat** is available at health food stores either raw or roasted. I recommend raw buckwheat, as roasted buckwheat is less nutritious, and may have a strong, burned flavor. Raw buckwheat cooks to a puffy, moist texture with an earthy, mild flavor.

• **Millet** is mostly used as birdseed in America. But, this nutritious grain feeds hundreds of millions of people around the world. It's a snap to prepare and easy to digest. Depending on the amount of water used, millet cooks light and fluffy, or moist and creamy.

• **Oats** are available in several forms. The most common of which is rolled oats. They are made from whole oats (also called oat groats) that are steamed until soft, then flattened into flakes between steel rollers, and then lightly toasted. These regular, "old-fashioned" rolled oats are used to make the dish we all know as "oatmeal."

Other oat forms include thick rolled oats, which lend a bit more chewiness to a dish (and crunchiness if made into granola). Whole oats resemble long-grain brown rice and are cooked much the same (i.e. cook 1 cup oat groats in 2 cups water for 1 hour). Expect a delightfully chewy and rich oaty flavor. Steel-cut (also called Irish or Scottish oats) and quick-cooking oats have undergone excessive processing, resulting in less-nourishing oat forms.

• **Quinoa** is a disk-shaped grain that unfurls a tiny tail when cooked. It's a mild, pleasant tasting grain, with a light and fluffy texture. Quinoa has the most protein of any grain and that protein is considered "complete" and of high-quality. Quinoa should be rinsed well to remove a natural bitter coating which may be present if the grains have not been thoroughly washed by the producer. By the way, the tiny tail mentioned above, is the germ.

• **Wild Rice** is an expensive grain that, when cooked with other grains, imparts an amazing nutty flavor and delightful chewiness. Cooked alone, it's a grain to savor with each bite.

Grains (refined)

Refined grains have had their germ and bran layers removed to extend shelf-life and reduce cooking time. Unfortunately, most of the nutrients are lost in the process. **White flour** results from whole wheat that's been completely refined. **Enriched white flour** has little of the vitamins and minerals and none of the fiber of whole wheat flour. **Couscous** is made from white flour. **Pearled barley** results from barley that's been highly refined—known as pearling. **Scotch** or **pot barley** has been refined (pearled), but not nearly to the extent as pearled barley. **Semolina** is the white flour remaining when whole durum wheat is refined.

White rice was originally brown rice until the bran and germ layers were removed, leaving only a starchy rump. **Hominy grits** are made from refined corn kernels. Less nourishing than its whole- grain counterparts, quick-cooking brown rice and quick-cooking oats have been cooked, dried, and packaged—resulting in nutrient loss.

Liquid Smoke

Just a small amount of this bottled liquid seasoning added to savory dishes will impart a light smoky flavor. Liquid smoke can be found in supermarkets near the ketchups and bar-b-q sauces. Look for brands that are free of artificial extracts and that contain only water and natural hickory smoke concentrate.

Maple Syrup (see Sweeteners)

Milk (non-dairy)

Health food stores carry the largest selection ever of non-dairy milks. Made variously of soybeans, grains, nuts, or coconut, the "milks" are fortified to equal or surpass the nutritional value of dairy milk. They can be used in any recipe calling for dairy milk and are free of cholesterol, lactose, and saturated animal fat.

As the flavors of these milks vary widely, it's best to sample a variety of non-dairy milks to find the right one. Better yet, try out any of the homemade versions included in this book before choosing.

Millet (see Grains, and Flours)

Mirin

Mirin is a naturally sweet, golden cooking wine made when rice and koji (a natural fermenting agent) are slowly brewed. Adding a small amount of mirin to stir-fries, dips, dressings, soups, or sauces will impart a mildly-sweet, ambrosial flavor—a classic Japanese touch. Look for a quality brand such as "Eden" at health food stores, and avoid cheaper, chemically brewed and artificially sweetened ones found in the mass markets.

Miso (see Soyfoods)

Mushrooms (dried)

Dried mushrooms are available packaged usually either sliced or in whole form. Before use, they should be soaked in boiling water for about 10 minutes and then added for further cooking to casseroles, soups, stews, or any other savory dish to add a rich, exquisite earthy flavor. My favorite is dried, sliced shiitake mushrooms. Store dried mushrooms in an airtight container in a cool spot for up to 6 months.

Non-Dairy Milk (see Milk)

Nori

Paper-thin, crisp sheets of dried sea vegetable generally used to enfold a cooked rice wrap—called sushi. Nori can be ground into flakes as a seasoning or added to a green salad for a "fishy" flavor.

If you purchase packaged nori that has not been toasted (will say so on package) it will be necessary to toast it before using in a recipe.

To toast nori, place nori sheets on baking sheet and bake 2 minutes at 300°. Nori will turn from purple-black (untoasted) to a bright green color with a crispy texture, when toasted. A toaster oven works fine.

Nutritional Yeast

Nutritional yeast, rich in vitamins, minerals, and protein, is made from single-cell organisms cultivated for use both as a nutritional supplement and as a seasoning. Available at health food stores, usually in the bulk bins, these tasty, golden-hued large flakes (or powder) can be added to pastas, soups, casseroles, or any dish to add a "cheesy" flavor.

A popular and widely available brand I recommend is "Red Star Vegetarian Support Formula," easily recognized by its bright yellow color and agreeable "cheesy" flavor. This product is made by growing and fermenting yeast on molasses. The yeast is harvested, washed, and then pasteurized and dried. As an inactive yeast, it has no leavening power nor does it promote Candida growth.

This product should not be confused with "brewer's yeast" which is a by-product of the brewing industry nor with "torula yeast" which is grown on wood waste products from the wood pulp industry. Both of these are sweetened and flavored due to their naturally bitter flavor. They do not contain the level of vitamins and minerals found in nutritional yeast. Nutritional yeast should be stored in an airtight container in a cool, dry spot for up to six months.

Oats (see Grains, and Flours)

Oils

Where do oils come from? The common oils originate from the following food sources:

beans	peanut oil, soy oil
nuts	almond oil, walnut oil
seeds	canola oil, sesame oil, flax oil, sunflower oil, safflower oil
grains	corn oil
fruits	olive oil, avocado oil, coconut oil

Look for oils that have been "expeller pressed" (check the label) since these oils are mechanically processed at relatively low temperatures without the use of chemicals. They must be refrigerated after opening to prevent rancidity. Rancid oil tastes bitter and causes a burning sensation in the throat. It usually has a strong, stale, soapy odor. Unless the label says "expeller" or "mechanically" pressed, the oil has undergone solvent extraction in which hexane (a toxic, petrochemical solvent) is used. Residues of hexane may remain in the oil, posing a possible health hazard.

Since high heat causes oil to decompose and degrade into potentially harmful compounds, it's prudent to limit the amount of stir frying, deep frying, and browning with oil. When you do choose to stir-fry with oil, use the least possible amount of oil (i.e. 1-2 teaspoons) and keep the cooking temperature at medium or low.

Better yet, use a small amount of coconut oil since it is a wholesome oil highly resistant to chemical changes when heated. In fact, due to its high saturated fat content, coconut oil is the safest (and most stable) oil to use when frying with oil.

• **Canola Oil** is known as a heart-healthy oil for its abundance of monounsaturated fat and beneficial omega-3 fatty acid profile. These fats, among other benefits, increase the body's "good" HDL cholesterol and decrease the "bad" LDL cholesterol.

Originally made from rapeseeds that contained significant levels of a toxic acid (erucic acid), canola oil is now made from a variety of rapeseed virtually free of erucic acid. Purchase canola oil that's been made organically since this forbids the use of genetically modified rapeseeds. Canola oil is the oil to go to when a no-taste or plain oil is called for in a recipe.

• **Coconut Oil** has long been mistakenly accused of being an unhealthy oil due to its high amount of saturated fat. However, current research shows that unlike saturated animal fat, coconut oil does not cause cardiovascular disease. In fact, coconut oil raises the body's good cholesterol (the kind that transports bad cholesterol out of the body).

Coconut oil is composed mostly of medium-chain fatty acids which the body metabolizes into energy, instead of storing as fat. Furthermore, the high amount of lauric acid found in coconut oil boosts immune function by playing a role in killing viruses, bacteria, fungi, yeasts, and other harmful microorganisms. It accomplishes this by dissolving the layer of fat that these disease-causing organisms construct to protect themselves from attack by the body's immune system.

In studies abroad, coconut oil is being investigated as a treatment for patients with AIDS. Preliminary research has revealed that coconut oil can effectively reduce both the quantity and vigor of the viral load in AIDS patients. This potent antiviral potential of coconut oil against HIV has been seen in AIDS patients who consumed approximately 3-4 tablespoons of coconut oil per day.

The only other food on earth that contains such an abundance of lauric acid—is human breast milk. Coconut milk and shredded coconut also contain lauric acid, but in smaller quantities. Coconut oil can easily be added to the diet as a replacement for the oil and fat currently used in or on foods. Since coconut oil is solid at room temperature, it can be softened or melted if briefly warmed up in a small pot.

• **Flax Seed Oil** is an excellent source of omega-3 fatty acids (actually it contains the essential fatty acid ALA, which the body converts to two other important fatty acids: DHA and EPA). Together these fatty acids play a critical role in the prevention and treatment of heart disease, rheumatoid arthritis, bowel disease, asthma, inflammatory conditions, and depression.

Studies show that as little as 1 tablespoon of flax oil daily can have, over time, dramatic effects. Other rich sources of the important ALA fatty acid include walnuts and flax seed meal. And, to a lesser, but still important, extent: canola oil, olive oil, hemp seeds, and hemp oil.

Flax oil has a golden color and pleasant buttery flavor when purchased "fresh." The oil is found in the refrigerator case of health food stores. Look on the side or bottom of the bottle for the pressing date. Don't buy the oil if the pressing date shows the oil to be older than 3 months (or it could taste "fishy" and be unpleasantly strong or bitter). Extra bottles of flax oil purchased can be stored in the freezer for 6 months. Or, refrigerate and use within 6 weeks of purchase.

Flax oil can be enjoyed on cooked grains, pasta, hot or cold veggies, popcorn, and in salad dressings. It should never be used in cooking, as its nutritional components would be destroyed.

• **Olive Oil** in bottles labeled "extra-virgin" indicates the oil was extracted from the first pressing of the olives. Extra-virgin olive oil, rich in heart-healthy monounsaturated fat, is too delicate to use in frying. Use it as a seasoning and in salad dressings, dips, and sauces. Make sure the oil comes packaged in an opaque or dark green glass bottle to protect it from the harsh store lights which degrade oils in clear glass bottles. Avoid oils sold in metal cans which can be contaminated with lead, plastic (from the plastic polymer can liner inside), or other contaminants.

To preserve olive oil, store it in the refrigerator after opening the bottle. A drawback to this is that the oil solidifies when chilled. For convenience, a small amount of the oil could be kept in a cool spot in the pantry for a short while and refilled as needed. All extra-virgin olive oils do not taste the same. In general, olives grown in cooler climates yield an oil with a distinctly spicy, pepper flavor, while those grown in milder climates result in oil that tastes mild and somewhat fruity.

• **Sesame Oil (toasted)** purchased at health food stores is usually of high quality and mellow flavor. Leave the chemicalized and harshly processed (and often bitter-tasting) supermarket and Asian store brands behind. Organic toasted sesame oil should indicate "expeller pressed" (a relatively low-temperature pressing process) and "unrefined" on the bottle for it to be of the highest quality.

Sesame seeds are roasted, then pressed to release the oil. A popular mild tasting product is "Spectrum" brand organic toasted sesame oil. It has a delightfully nutty flavor and aroma and will add a pleasing depth of flavor to a dish, not overwhelm it. Store the bottle in the refrigerator after opening, where it will keep for up to 3 months.

Olive Oil (see Oils)

Organic

Organic foods are grown without the use of toxic chemicals and fertilizers, and processed without genetic modification or irradiation (terms defined later). Most of the foods grown and processed at present in the United States are "conventionally grown" using toxic pesticides, fungicides, or chemical fertilizers. Studies show that residues of these poisons remain on and in the food and may pose health dangers.

If organic produce is not available, buy fruits and vegetables with skins that can be peeled. This helps avoid the surface contaminants (although it does not remedy the pesticides absorbed through a plant's root system).

Foods organically grown and processed are not allowed to have been genetically modified nor subjected to irradiation. Foods that have been genetically modified have had genes inserted into them for the purposes of improving flavor and texture, and increasing yields and disease and pesticide resistance. The genes that are spliced into the fruit, vegetable, bean, grain, seed, or nut plants could originate from bacteria or plants—or from insects, animals, and even humans.

According to the laws of nature, genetic material from a pig, for example, could never combine naturally with genetic material of a soybean. Yet, biotechnologists are doing such combining and many people find that abhorrent, whether for personal, cultural, ethical, or religious reasons. Some fear that we are introducing completely unknown substances into the food supply and that we have crossed a barrier never meant to traverse.

Foods that have been irradiated have been exposed to radiation (from radioactive nuclear waste) in an effort to extend shelf life and kill insects, parasites, or bacteria lurking in the foods. While the foods subjected to irradiation may not actually become radioactive, they are being exposed to doses up to millions of times stronger than a standard chest x-ray. This is enough exposure to alter the chemical bonds that hold plant molecules together, creating new arrangements which we humans have never consumed in our long history on the planet.

Young children especially are sensitive to pesticides because a given amount of a pesticide has a greater impact on a small body than on a large, adult body. Also, kids suffer more from pesticides because these toxic chemicals initiate cancer more easily in a child's rapidly dividing cells than in the dormant cells of an adult.

Pasta (whole-grain and gluten-free)

Purchase only those pastas that are made of 100% whole grains as refined flour pastas are deficient in a host of areas. Tasty, gluten-free whole-grain pastas are widely available and include those made from brown rice, quinoa, corn, and buckwheat. Their textures and flavors are superb and they are as easy to cook and work with as traditional wheat flour pastas.

Quinoa (see Grains)

Rolled Oats (see Grains, and Flours)

Salt

Sea salt is made from evaporated sea water. Some brands are minimally refined and contain trace minerals; others are made at high temperatures and devoid of minerals.

Table salt results from high heat and chemical processes used to purify salt obtained from salt mines. Most brands of sea and table salt mix in anti-caking agents (calcium silicate) to keep the salt from clumping. The addition of iodine (potassium iodide) ensures the elimination of a disease that swells the thyroid (goiter). And, a sugar (dextrose) is added to keep the iodine from oxidizing and turning the salt yellow.

Kosher salt refers to salt (either from the sea or salt mines) that is ground into large, "fluffy" grains that don't clump, and that stick well to foods. Kosher salt that's called for in a recipe can be replaced with ½ as much sea or table salt.

Sesame Oil (see Oils)

Shoyu (see Soyfoods)

Stevia (see Sweeteners)

Soy Milk, Soy Sauce, Soy Yogurt (see Soyfoods)

Soyfoods

Soybeans can be turned into a wide variety of traditional products, including soy milk, tofu, tempeh, miso, soy sauce, yogurt, and edamame. The soybean is the only legume providing complete protein, meaning it provides all eight essential amino acids that the body requires for health and maintenance.

As meat alternatives, soyfoods like tofu and tempeh are important sources of protein for hundreds of millions of people worldwide. Soyfoods are rich in compounds called phytoestrogens or isoflavones, which are plant-based estrogens capable of exerting powerful, health-promoting effects.

Unfortunately, some people avoid soy in the mistaken belief that soy estrogens somehow increase cancer risk. However, the latest studies confirm what's been known for decades. Namely, that soyfoods actually decrease the risk of a variety of cancers—including both estrogen-receptor positive and estrogen-receptor negative cancers.

A major study in 2009, as reported in the *Journal of the American Medical Association* (2009;302:2437-43), found that women being treated for breast cancer had much less risk of cancer returning or of dying from cancer if they included traditional soy products in their daily diet. That same year, two new papers published in the *American Journal of Clinical Nutrition* (2009;89:1145-1163,1920-1926) found that the consumption of traditional soyfoods reduces the risk of breast cancer and prostate cancer.

A 2009 study conducted by the National Cancer Institute concluded that the consumption of traditional soy products in childhood are associated with a lower risk of breast cancer later in life. Another study in the previous year in *Nutrition Journal* (June 3, 2008;7:17) reported that traditional soy products were completely safe for breast cancer patients.

Soy estrogens mimic a woman's own natural estrogen hormones by attaching themselves to the body's hormone receptor sites on cells. This effectively blocks actual estrogens—powerful growth hormones—from attaching to the cells and fueling cancer growth. These unattached estrogens move on and are eliminated by the body. With lower levels of estrogens in their bodies, women have reduced risk of breast cancer. And, this applies to men who eat soyfoods. They too have a reduced risk (and better outcome) of prostate cancer, a hormone-related cancer.

Soy estrogens are also responsible for decreasing bad cholesterol, and increasing good cholesterol; for reducing the risk of heart attack and stroke; for reducing arterial plaque build-up; for decreasing high blood pressure and for improving bone, brain, and nerve cell function. And for helping to relieve symptoms of menopause.

These impressive health benefits have been confirmed in people eating the following traditional soyfoods—not from the use of concentrated isoflavone supplements or from "fake meats" (meat-like products made of highly-processed soy protein isolate).

• **Edamame** is a Japanese name for green soybeans. Eaten straight from their pods or already shelled, edamame (eh-dah-MAH-meh) are buttery, finger foods that can be quite addictive. After green soybeans are harvested, they're cooked and usually frozen. At home, cook them as you would other frozen vegetables (instructions are on each bag) and eat as is, or added to salads, stir-fries, and soups.

• **Miso** is a salty seasoning, with a pasty texture, made of fermented soybeans. It adds an enhanced flavor to any dish. Miso manufacturers make it by mixing cooked soybeans with salt, water, and cultured grains. This mixture is then fermented from several months to one year—depending on the type of miso desired.

Misos fermented a shorter time contain less salt and result in light-colored, sweet misos that add a delicate, slightly sweet touch to mashed potatoes, light sauces, and chowders; longer-fermented misos are salted more and yield brown or red dark misos which deliver rich and hearty flavors to soups, stews, gravies, salad dressings, and other dishes.

The question of whether or not salt raises blood pressure has long been controversial. But, what is known, is that despite miso's saltiness (a 2 teaspoon serving of miso, on average, contains about $1/6$ teaspoon salt), eating miso may actually lower your blood pressure. During miso's fermentation process, potent amino acids (peptides) are created. These act to block the action of an enzyme that elevates blood pressure.

Miso can be found in small plastic tubs in the refrigerator section of health food stores. Look for miso that's unpasteurized—it's loaded with beneficial bacteria and enzymes. It will keep in the refrigerator for several months, at least.

• **Soy Milk** can be made in several ways. Whether commercially prepared or homemade, the basics are the same. Dried soybeans are soaked overnight. Then the beans are cooked, blended, and strained to yield a rich, non-dairy product. It's an excellent substitute for dairy milk and free of cholesterol and saturated animal fat.

A relatively fresh soy milk is available in milk cartons in the store's refrigerated dairy case. Soy milk also is available unrefrigerated in shelf-stable boxes. The various brands of "fresh" and unrefrigerated soy milks taste surprisingly different and I recommend trying a few.

• **Soy Sauce** that's found in supermarkets is usually made from chemically defatted soybeans that have been treated with petroleum solvents and hydrochloric acid. It's no wonder that these excessively salty and additive-loaded brands can taste sharp and disagreeable when compared with the naturally fermented Japanese soy sauces known as shoyu and tamari. Naturally brewed combinations of soybeans, salt, and water, these traditional soy sauces offer rich and complex flavors—what you'd expect from a 1-2 year aging process.

Shoyu and tamari may be used interchangeably, although connoisseurs prefer that tamari be used in a dish during cooking, and that shoyu be added after cooking. For those people choosing to avoid wheat, tamari is wheat-free, but shoyu is fermented with wheat. Best to check the label on the bottle. Store these soy sauces after opening in the refrigerator where they'll keep for several months.

• **Soy Yogurt** Made of soy milk and active cultures ("friendly bacteria"), soy yogurt has the flavor, consistency, and nutritional profile of dairy yogurt, but without any cholesterol or saturated animal fat. Available plain and fruit-flavored, soy yogurt can be used and enjoyed in the same ways as dairy yogurt. Look for it at health food stores usually next to the dairy yogurt.

• **Tempeh** is relatively low in calories, high in protein and fiber, and without a drop of cholesterol. It is as fine a meat substitute as you'll find. It's made from cooked whole soybeans that have been cultured and incubated for 18-24 hours. The result is a thick, flat soybean cake held together by cottony white threads (courtesy of the culture used to process the soybeans). Tempeh (pronounced TEM-pay) has a chewy texture and a mild, mushroomy flavor.

Tempeh is found in the refrigerator section of health food stores. Check the expiration date stamped on the package and try to purchase tempeh as many weeks as possible before the expiration date.

The "older" the tempeh, the riper and stronger the flavor. It's best to store tempeh at home in the freezer (it'll keep for 3 months) to slow the ripening process and better preserve tempeh's mild flavor.

When grated, temeph can be used in dishes calling for ground meat. It can be added to stir-fries, spaghetti sauce, pizza, chili, and made into savory burgers. Don't be alarmed by any black or gray spots that may form on the tempeh cakes. These are natural mold growths that won't cause any harm. However, toss out the tempeh if it develops a strong, foul odor or has mold spots of other colors. The quality, texture, and flavor of tempeh can vary dramatically between the many brands available. Try them all to find the one that works best for you.

• **Tofu** is a highly nutritious and digestible soyfood (often called "bean curd") made from soy milk in much the same way that cheese is made from cow's milk. A natural mineral coagulant is added to soy milk which causes curds to form. The curds are gathered and pressed to create blocks of tofu.

Tofu is available in either soft or firm varieties. Soft tofu contains far more water and much less protein than does firm tofu, and for that reason I recommend firm and extra-firm tofus. These tofus keep their shape in cooking and are better suited than soft tofu for stir-fry dishes, scrambled "eggs," casseroles, and sandwich fillers. And, wherever soft tofu is called for, such as in spreads, desserts, smoothies, and sauces, firm tofu works equally well.

There can be great variance between the different brands of firm and extra-firm tofus. Check the nutrition panel on the package. I prefer tofus that have 10 or more grams of protein per 3-ounce serving, as I find them enjoyably "firm." The higher the number of protein grams per 3-ounce serving, the firmer the tofu. The really firm tofus are dense and chewy, and hold up quite well in stir-fries, soups, and on the grill.

You'll find tofu usually sold in water in sealed plastic packages. Check the "expiration date" to get the freshest tofu possible. Refrigerate the tofu until ready for use. Store any leftover, uncooked pieces of tofu in cold water in a sealed container in the refrigerator. It will stay "fresh" for about 7-10 days, provided the water is changed at least every other day or so.

You can give tofu a complete make-over by freezing it. Its texture will become spongy and chewy after it's thawed. To freeze tofu, remove the tofu from its package. Then rinse, and place the tofu on a plate or tray. Leave it as a block or cut into slices. Freeze overnight or at least 4-6 hours and keep in the freezer in a covered container.

To thaw frozen tofu, place the tofu in a baking dish in a 350° oven, for 15-20 minutes. When cool, the tofu can be pressed between your hands to remove excess water. It's now ready to be cubed, chunked, or crumbled, and added to any number of dishes. This thawed tofu will absorb the flavor of vegetables, herbs, spices, and other seasonings exceptionally well.

In recipes that call for 16-ounces of tofu, feel free to use a 14-ounce package of tofu if that's all you have. It will work satisfactorily well. A final note: If you're planning to use tofu in a dish that involves no cooking, such as in smoothies or dips, the tofu should be cut in several pieces and boiled in water for 5 minutes to kill any bacteria that may be present in the tofu.

Sweeteners

Since all sugars, even the "good" ones, have so few nutrients in relation to their calories, it's advised to use them all as sparingly as possible. Choose minimally-processed sweeteners, and those that are organic, if you can, since sugar-processing concentrates toxic chemicals at each stage of production.

• **Agave Nectar** is a natural liquid sweetener made from the juice of a cactus-like plant from Mexico. It is an acceptable alternative to honey as it dissolves easily, and has a sweet and mild flavor. Also, agave does not spike blood sugar levels as excessively as do the refined sugars.

• **Artificial Sweeteners** include saccharin (Sweet'N Low), sucralose (Splenda), and aspartame (NutraSweet and Equal). These potent chemical compounds are up to 600 times sweeter than sugar and have been blamed for medical complaints ranging from aberrant psychological behavior to physical damage of brain and liver cells. Far from satisfying, these sweeteners seem to increase hunger (and calorie intake!) and cravings for sweets.

Other artificial sweeteners include the "sugar alcohols." Among them are sorbitol (highly processed from corn syrup and a possible cause of intestinal disorders), mannitol (synthetically made from corn sugar and associated with kidney and intestinal disease), and xylitol (naturally found in some fruits and vegetables, but commercially derived from wood chips and other non-nutritive materials using significant amounts of energy and chemicals). Diseases of the kidney and bladder are associated with xylitol consumption in commercially-prepared food products.

• **Blackstrap Molasses** is the most nutritious and rich-tasting of the various molasses forms. It is a by-product of the refining of sugar cane and sugar beets. The juice of these plants is boiled and sugar crystals form in the process. These crystals are removed to be processed into sugar. The dark liquid that remains is blackstrap molasses. Unlike all other sugars, it's high in calcium and iron and adds a rich, assertive flavor to any dish.

• **Brown Rice Syrup** is a golden-colored syrup with a faint flavor of butterscotch. It's made by grinding brown rice into a meal, cooking it, then adding a natural culture to break down the rice's starches into natural sugars. The liquid is extracted, then cooked until it thickens into a syrup. It's about half as sweet as sugar and can be used in place of any liquid sweetener. However, since brown rice syrup leaves a bit of an "aftertaste" for some people, I suggest using brown rice syrup in combination with maple syrup or agave nectar.

• **Evaporated Cane Juice** is made from sugar cane juice that is filtered, dehydrated, and milled into a golden powder. Containing some trace of the vitamins and minerals of the original sugar cane, evaporated cane juice can be used in place of white sugar, measure for measure. A much darker version has a rich molasses taste and can be used to replace brown sugar.

• **Fructose** is a simple sugar that is naturally found in fruit. The "fructose" used to sweeten beverages, baked goods, desserts, condiments, and many other foods is not made from fruit, as it would be unprofitable to extract it. This commercial fructose is available in several forms. One is high-fructose corn syrup (HFCS) which is made from cornstarch that's been treated with acidic chemicals to convert the starch into sugar. This makes HFCS an even less natural product than totally-refined cornstarch.

Another type of fructose is available in a dry or crystal form. Made from highly processed beet and cane sugar, it is promoted as a healthy sweetener. However, the excessive use of commercial fructose sweeteners—not hard to do when you think how many foods are loaded with them—can dramatically increase a person's triglycerides (the fats found in the blood) and "bad" LDL cholesterol. These are serious heart-disease risks.

Unlike regular sugar, much of which goes directly into the bloodstream, fructose is entirely sent to the liver for metabolism. The high amount of refined fructose being consumed, no matter what the source, puts a severe strain on the liver's ability to function normally. Most nutrition experts advise people to read food labels and stay away from commercial fructose-sweetened foods.

• **Maple Syrup** results when maple tree sap is boiled down to a fraction of its original volume. Avoid "maple-flavored" or "pancake" syrups since these are nothing more than refined corn syrups with artificial coloring and flavoring. Organic maple syrup is free of the formaldehyde, chemical antifoaming agents, and mold inhibitors used by many U.S. producers. Refrigerate maple syrup after opening, to keep it from fermenting.

Generally, the lighter the color of maple syrup, the milder the maple flavor. The darker-colored maple syrups have rich strong maple flavor. Both light and dark maple syrups—even "Grade B" (the darkest and strongest-flavored)—are equally good for table use, cooking, and baking. The light syrups are made from first-of-the-season sap flows, while the darker ones are made much later in the season.

• **Stevia** is a sweetener derived from the leaves of a South American plant (although now cultivated widely in Asia). While the Japanese have long used stevia as a sugar replacement, the lack of extensive safety trials in the U.S. has given this sweetener a controversial image. What is not in dispute is that stevia does not affect blood sugar or cause tooth decay. It's also calorie-free.

Stevia comes in several forms. The finely-powdered, dried stevia leaves have a greenish color and licorice flavor. White stevia powder is intensely-sweet (as little as ½ teaspoon can equal 1 cup of sugar in sweetness!) Stevia concentrate is a black syrupy liquid (with 3-4 drops equalling 1 teaspoon of sugar's sweetening power).

Many cooks prefer to use stevia in conjunction with another natural sweetener, such as maple syrup, fruit juice concentrates, etc. This hides any licorice flavor or slight bitter aftertaste associated with stevia.

Tahini

Tahini is a thick, creamy paste made by grinding hulled sesame seeds. It's available raw or roasted, and buying organic tahini will ensure that no chemical solvents were used to dehull the sesame seeds prior to grinding. Raw tahini has a mild, almost sweet flavor, while roasted tahini has a deep, rich flavor. Tahini can be used instead of butter on toast, and in smoothies, and thinned with water for adding to stir-fries, sauces, desserts, steamed vegetables, dressings, and other dishes. After opening, refrigerate tahini (and all other naturally made seed and nut butters) to keep it from getting rancid.

Tamari (see Soyfoods)

Tapioca

Tapioca is made from the root of the cassava plant and is commonly available either as quick-cooking granules or small pearls. Generally, the granules thicken a simmering dish in 15 minutes, while the pearls need 25-30 minutes. If you need granules, but only have pearls, you can grind the pearls in a blender to make quick-cooking tapioca. Tapioca-thickened dishes have a pleasant chewy texture not present with powdered starch thickeners.

Tempeh (see Soyfoods)

Tofu (see Soyfoods)

Tomatoes (sun-dried)
Ripe, tomato halves that have been either dried in the sun, or more likely, oven-dried. Available packed in oil or dry-packed in bags—and sometimes in the bulk containers at health food stores. I recommend the dry (and organic) form. These have to be rehydrated before use by soaking in just-boiled water for about 10 minutes. Then they're ready to be chopped and added for further cooking to casseroles, soups, sauces, and many other savory dishes to lend a sweet, roasted, and intense tomato flavor. Any unused dry-packed, sun-dried tomatoes can be stored in an airtight container in a cool spot for up to 6 months.

Wild Rice (see Grains)

Yogurt (see Soyfoods)

Recommended Resources

Books

Barnard, Neal (M.D.). *Foods That Fight Pain*, 1998.

Barnard, Neal (M.D.). *Dr. Neal Barnard's Program for Reversing Diabetes*, 2007

Barnard, Neal (M.D.). *21-Day Weight Loss Kickstart*, 2011

Braly, James (M.D.). *Dangerous Grains*, 2002.

Campbell, T. Colin (Ph.D.). *The China Study*, 2004.

Davis, Brenda (RD) and Melina, Vesanto (MS, RD). *Becoming Vegan: The Complete Guide to Adopting a Healthy Plant-Based Diet*, 2000.

Esselstyn, Caldwell (M.D.). *Prevent and Reverse Heart Disease*, 2007.

Gabbe Day, Wendy. *Scatter Vegan Sweets*, 2011.

Green, Peter (M.D.). *Celiac Disease*, 2007.

Klaper, Michael (M.D.). *Pregnancy, Children and The Vegan Diet*, 1991.

Klaper, Michael (M.D.). *Vegan Nutrition: Pure and Simple*, 1999.

McDougall, John (M.D.). *Dr. McDougall's Digestive Tune-Up*, 2006.

Newkirk, Ingrid E. *Making Kind Choices: Everyday Ways to Enhance Your Life and Avoid Cruelty to Animals*, 2004

Physicians Committee For Responsible Medicine. *Healthy Eating For Life* (Series), 2002.

Roberts, Holly (D.O.). *Your Vegetarian Pregnancy*, 2003.

Stepaniak, Joanne (MS Ed.). *The Vegan Sourcebook*, 1998.

Stepaniak, Joanne (MS Ed.). *Raising Vegetarian Children*, 2002.

Wasserman, Debra and Mangels, Reed (Ph.D.). *Simply Vegan*, 2006

National Organizations

American Vegan Society, P.O Box 369, Malaga, NJ 08328. (856)694-2887. www.americanvegan.org

North American Vegetarian Society, P.O. Box 72, Dolgeville, NY 13329. (518)568-7970. www.navs-online.org

People for the Ethical Treatment of Animals (PETA), 501 Front St., Norfolk, VA 23510. (757)622-7382. www.peta.org

Physicians Committee for Responsible Medicine (PCRM), 5100 Wisconsin Ave., N.W. #404, Washington, D.C. 20016. (202)686-2210. www.pcrm.org

Vegetarian Resource Group, P.O. Box 1463, Baltimore, MD 21203. (410)366-8343. www.vrg.org

Index

French: Dressing 66, Onion Dip 84, toast 42
'fried': 'egg' sandwich 126, tofu 'egg' rice 128
frostings: cashew 151, chocolate 152, chocolate date 152, cinnamon maple 151, fruit butter 142, oat cream 36, orange maple 151, 'whipped cream' 153
fructose 180
Fruit Butter 142
Fruity 'Jell-o' 142

G

garbanzo bean flour 164
Garbanzo 'Tuna' Salad 56
garbo: bars 47, burgers 118, 'nuts' 100
Garbo Rounds 48
garlic, roasted 91
genetic modification 173-74
Ginger: Juice 92, tea 34
glazes, maple: cinnamon 151, orange 151
gluten 165-66
gluten-free: flours 164-65, grains 167, pasta 174
grains: cooking 25-27, whole 167-68, refined 168
granola, flax-date 43
Greek Yellow Split Pea Dip 83
Green Goddess Dressing 65
greens, storing 127
'guacamole', broccoli 81
guide, daily healthy eating 10

H

hash, tempeh 131
herbs 120, and spices 118, freezing 117
high fructose corn syrup 180
Homemade Flour: Buckwheat 28, Millet 28, Oat 28
'Honey' Mustard Dressing 65
'Horchata' 39
Hot Chocolate 36
Hummus 78, roasted red pepper 78

I

Instant: 'Chicken' Broth 111, Nut Milk 32
iron 20, 21
irradiation 173-74
Israeli Salad 59

J

'jell-o', fruity 142

K

Kasha Krunch Cereal 42
Ketchup 87
Kimchi Express 60
kitchen, equipping vegan 16
kosher salt 175

L

'lasagna': navy 104, spinach 104
'lassis': banana-strawberry 40, cucumber 40
lauric acid 171-72
Lemon Coconut Tofu 'Cheesecake' 136
lemon juice 64
Lemon: Parsley Dressing 63, Tofu 'Pound Cake' 148
lentils: about 161, cooking 24, dal 108, dip 82, pâté 82, soup 111
lignans 163
liquid smoke 169

M

Mac & 'Cheese' 74
'macaroons', chocolate chip 155
Mango Salsa 80
maple syrup 180-81
Maple: Glazes 151, Noodle Pudding 140, Tahini Dressing 64
'Margaritas' 39
'mayonnaise', tofu 85
measurement chart 191
'meatballs', tempeh 120
'meatloaf', tempeh 98
melts, 'cheese' 72-73
menus, sample 12

A Pound of Apples Is How Many Grams?

In America, we measure things using the English system, while much of the world uses the Metric System. We measure length by the **foot**, they use the **meter**. We measure volume with the **cup** (and **spoons**), they use the **liter**. And, finally, the **pound** tells us how much things weigh, while the **gram** tells the rest of the world the same.

The following chart compares some common units of measurement using English and Metric units (some slightly rounded for easier conceptualizing):

English	Metric
4 cups (1 quart)	1 liter
1 gallon (4 quarts)	4 liters
1 ounce	28 grams
3½ ounces	100 grams
1 pound	454 grams
2¼ pounds	1 kilogram

Some Other Equivalents

1 tablespoon = 3 teaspoons

2 tablespoons = ¹/₈ cup = 1 fluid ounce

16 tablespoons = 1 cup = 8 fluid ounces = ½ pint

1 quart = 4 cups = 32 fluid ounces = 2 pints

About the Author

David Gabbe is the author of a number of previous books, including *From David's Pure Vegetarian Kitchen*, *The Going Vegetarian Cookbook*, and *Why Do Vegetarians Eat Like That?* He teaches plant-based cooking and nutrition in Oregon and Washington (since 1990) and has been a speaker at numerous seminars and conferences on the West Coast.